WRONG LANES
HAVE RIGHT
TURNS

WRONG LANES HAVE RIGHT TURNS

A Pardoned Man's Escape from the School-to-Prison Pipeline and What We Can Do to Dismantle It

———

MICHAEL PHILLIPS

WATERBROOK

Published in the United States by WaterBrook, an imprint of Random House, a division of Penguin Random House LLC.

WATERBROOK® and its deer colophon are registered trademarks of Penguin Random House LLC.

Library of Congress Cataloging-in-Publication Data
Names: Phillips, Michael (Pastor), author.
Title: Wrong lanes have right turns : a pardoned man's escape from the school-to-prison pipeline and what we can do to dismantle it / Michael Phillips.
Description: First edition. | [Colorado Springs, Colorado] : WaterBrook, [2022] | Includes bibliographical references.
Identifiers: LCCN 2021028714 | ISBN 9780593193907 (hardcover) | ISBN 9780593193914 (ebook)
Subjects: LCSH: Phillips, Michael (Pastor) | African American clergy—Biography. | Christian biography—United States. | Ex-convicts—United States—Biography. | African American boys—Education—Social aspects. | Racism in education—United States. | Prison-industrial complex—United States. | Educational change—United States.
Classification: LCC BR1725.P493 A3 2022 | DDC 270.092 [B]—dc23
LC record available at https://lccn.loc.gov/2021028714

Printed in Canada on acid-free paper

waterbrookmultnomah.com

2 4 6 8 9 7 5 3 1

First Edition

Title-page prison image by Carles Rabada on Unsplash, and title-page school image by Kyo Azuma on Unsplash
Chapter-number and space-break "u-turn" images: copyright © iStock.com/bgblue

Book design by Victoria Wong

SPECIAL SALES Most WaterBrook books are available at special quantity discounts when purchased in bulk by corporations, organizations, and special-interest groups. Custom imprinting or excerpting can also be done to fit special needs. For information, please email specialmarketscms@penguinrandomhouse.com.

*For my father, Richard Wellington Phillips.
You modeled manhood, love for family,
service to community, and moral courage for
social justice. Your love for humanity and
faith in God is my greatest inheritance.*

Contents

Prologue

We all share a similar story, but the difference in the details makes us believe we're not the same.

In 2012 my eyes were opened to a collective story unfolding in my city. As the pastor of an amazing church in the great city of Baltimore, I was asked to convene a meeting with local faith leaders to better connect with some of our local schools. At that meeting, our host, the Maryland Campaign for Achievement Now (MarylandCAN), shared data that stunned me. Examining the National Assessment of Educational Progress (NAEP) scores that broke down the demographics of our city schools, I learned that out of approximately eighty-six thousand students, 46 percent were African American males. Of that group, only 9 percent were proficient in reading.

Nine percent.

That meant *91 percent* of Black males were not reading at their proper grade level. At first, I couldn't believe it. It was inconceivable to me.

The report did not focus solely on deficiencies; it also focused on hope and community. And the data informed us of schools that were defying the odds. The report called these Opportunity Schools because they afforded students from both low-income households and higher-income households the opportunity to succeed. "Seven public elementary school programs and one public middle school program . . . repeatedly [led] children from low-income families to outperform overall state proficiency rates."

I left the meeting shocked and a little jaded. I was frustrated about how the opportunity gap for kids in certain locations is so massive, and I wondered how we were trying—if at all—to close that gap. But what was clear was that we can't close the gap in achievement without closing the gap in opportunity. If kids don't have opportunity, what difference does achievement make?

That was the day I altered course and began advocating for change in education. I wish it was the same day that the change countless children and families were hoping for became a reality, but systemic modification takes time. It also takes policy transformation. While serving on the Maryland State Board of Education, I made another course correction toward reimagining education. At a teacher appreciation dinner, I was seated at the same table as the chief executive officer of Baltimore City Public Schools. So during dinner I leaned over to ask her a question burning in my mind.

"What would it look like," I asked, "if somebody intentionally took on some of your lowest-performing schools with the intention of turning them around? What if they created a network among those schools? What would that look like in partnership with the district—would you even be interested in something like that?"

Without a blink, she simply asked, "When do you want to get started?"

"I'll get started right away," I replied.

And with that invitation, a journey began. I began to visit local schools. I wanted to know how they worked—and how we could replicate successes across our city without replicating what *wasn't* working. I then began to tour schools that were doing well at giving kids from low-income households an opportunity to succeed. Not just tours in Baltimore, by the way, but tours all over the United States. I went just about everywhere to see what was working and how other districts were addressing the challenges we faced. As I saw the odds against the project, it made me only more determined. *It's gonna have to work,* I decided. *We have to figure it out.*

You see, I knew that this was not just an education issue. For many kids, it was a survival issue. Schools are never just schools. Statistics never tell the full story, but seeing the raw data on those educational reports was not just a rallying cry for me to act. It was a reminder of how very different my life nearly was.

I realized I was staring into my own story—the story of a young soul turned around, but just barely, because of a second chance at education. I had almost been just another statistic. My feverish work in trying to solve a problem that was putting young men and women at chaotic intersections was a result of once being at one myself.

I knew I was part of another story, another group of young men that seemed predestined to have a location set for them: on the street corners or behind prison bars. I had accepted that world and the familiar narrative it often brings.

But one day in 1993, as I was speeding south toward Richmond and closing in on that chaotic intersection between I-95 and I-64, I received a phone call from my mother that changed my story. She asked me to come back home, and even though I knew this was putting me right in harm's way, I knew it was the right thing to do.

At that intersection I chose to make the right turn.

This book is the story of how one life turned around. I want to share it with you because I believe we're all at our own intersections of what is possible and what is purposeful. But if we don't make the right turns, we might not reach our destinations. My story, in more than one way, is about school—the ways it doesn't work for everyone and the ways I dream it can. As you read the story of one young man's experience, I pray you'll take from it the principles and passion that *any* of us can use to change the world of a child or a classroom for the better, right where we are.

Prologue

Just look at the headlines. Or the statistics. Or the eyes of kids in classrooms all over America. Maybe we're all headed in the wrong direction right now. But I have good news.

You see, I'm living proof that even wrong lanes have right turns.

WRONG LANES
HAVE RIGHT
TURNS

CHAPTER ONE

My Soul Looks Back and Wonders

Hold fast to dreams
For if dreams die
Life is a broken-winged bird
That cannot fly.

—Langston Hughes

My childhood dreams resembled red construction paper pasted on white cardboard. I can still picture a little report I made for career day in first grade. We had to show our class what profession we wanted to have—who we thought we could eventually become when we grew up. For me there was no question. I wanted to be a lawyer.

My mother and grandmother had inspired this ambition by regularly watching *Perry Mason* reruns on CBS. The black-and-white television show starred Raymond Burr as a brilliant defense lawyer working in Los Angeles. Each episode involved a different crime and trial and was memorably named after a case, such as "The Case of the Moth-Eaten Mink" and "The Case of the Polka Dot Pony." The mystery of every plot and the creative ways Perry Mason battled for justice ignited my young mind. I would watch, riveted. I daydreamed about walking into a courtroom under a sharp fedora. *I could be a smooth lawyer like Perry one day,* I felt.

I've always been a dreamer. I grew up in Baltimore's Park Heights, son of a working middle-class family. Our duplex didn't have much of a yard. My father was a full-time pastor *and* somehow a full-time truck driver; my mother worked for the Maryland state lottery until she decided to stay at home full-time with me and my three siblings.

I had every right to dream, and Park Heights made dreaming easy. I loved my neighborhood. Every corner was lively, each with its distinct sound. On one corner you could hear the trash talk of old men playing checkers outside the rowhouses; then just a block down the street, you could hear hip-hop music coming from someone's stoop with young men arguing over a game of dice. I was inspired by those simple echoes. But sometimes the beautiful noise was silenced by the crashing cries that came from other corners in my neighborhood—corners that weren't so safe. Cries of crime and violence. Those dueling reverberations were normal where I grew up. Kids played outside either until the streetlamps came on . . . or until sirens sent everyone indoors.

Though we inevitably had rough elements to deal with, such as the drug corners around us, the addicts that occupied them, or the violence that took place—sometimes right in front of us—I still didn't have a problem dreaming big. In those clattering moments, I would sit in my grandmother's kitchen, sneaking too-hot bites of some of her famous gumbo from the pot bubbling on the stove, and listen to her talk about her heroes.

My grandmother loved not only watching *Perry Mason* on television but also talking about a *real* lawyer from Baltimore. Thurgood Marshall studied law at Howard University and graduated first in his class. After Howard, Marshall opened a private practice firm in Baltimore. He was the first African American member of the U.S. Supreme Court and served on it for twenty-four years until 1991. He also just so happened to have grown up not so far away from Park Heights.

In 1954, while chief counsel for the National Association for the Advancement of Colored People (NAACP), Thurgood Marshall served as chief attorney in a landmark case before the Supreme Court. It was one of the greatest and most meaningful court decisions in US history. Simply, *Brown v. Board of Education* declared that racial segregation in public schools was unconstitutional. It became one of the cornerstones of the civil rights movement, beginning a new—but still deeply complicated—period in American life.

For almost six decades, the Supreme Court's ruling in

Plessy v. Ferguson (1896) had made it legal to have racially segregated public facilities as long as the facilities were "equal" for both Blacks and Whites. This would become known as the "separate but equal" doctrine. *Brown v. Board of Education* overturned this ideology. During the arguments for the case, Marshall was asked what he meant by *equal,* and he quickly replied, "Equal means getting the same thing, at the same time, and in the same place."

Those are the words of a hero. Thurgood Marshall gave me a model for success, something to believe in when I was still too young to realize the odds against me and too naïve to know the hard road ahead.

Marshall was solid proof that dreams could happen. But he also knew what it took to achieve them. As he once explained, "A man can make what he wants of himself if he truly believes that he must be ready for hard work and many heartbreaks."

Little did I know that on the day I would be declaring to my first-grade class my dream of following in Thurgood Marshall's footsteps, I would experience the latter part of that formula for success.

Heartbreak.

I often hated going to school. This was not because of the learning but because of the fighting. It was a good day if I got from home to school and back again without punches thrown.

No one likes being forced to fight, but in our neighborhood, you learned quickly that if you didn't stand up for yourself, you would perpetually be picking yourself up off the ground.

One reason guys picked fights with me in the first place was because of the way Mom dressed us. She made me wear sweaters and collared shirts to school. Not cool, Mom. I looked like a little doctor walking into the classroom. This was *not* a good thing for a first grader who was already a quiet kid. I looked different, "smart." And that was the *last* thing any of us kids in Park Heights wanted. Just at a glance, the very idea that I might be intellectually curious prompted other kids to want to punch my enlightened face.

My elementary school was a little over a mile from our house. I walked there, along with my sister and other classmates. We didn't think anything about the blight we saw, the occasional needles we had to step over, or the homeless people we passed. The city sidewalks littered with broken bottles and occupied with interesting characters weren't the things I dreaded. The fighting didn't matter. It was the school itself.

The place felt more like a prison than a school, with small, crowded rooms and cage-like bars over the windows and doors. A predominantly White staff oversaw our crowded all-Black student body. Sometimes it seemed that our principal and teachers were more like a warden and guards whose real job was just to keep us there until the bell finally rang and our time was served.

My first-grade teacher was Miss Battle, and I will never

forget her. She was a surly woman who seemed to have already made up her mind about me before we ever met. On the first day of class, she placed me in the back of the classroom. A kid named Dontae Eliot sat right next to me. Picture the character of Pigpen from Charlie Brown (you know, the kid always surrounded by a cloud of bugs and dust). Dontae Eliot *smelled,* and I had to experience his aroma every single day. He also thought he was some sort of black-belt martial artist, so he was constantly trying to do Bruce Lee–style kicks on me. We regularly got into it, and Miss Battle always had to break it up.

Our teacher couldn't distinguish between one student looking like a little lawyer and the other resembling a homeless kid from the street. It didn't matter that Dontae was loud and obnoxious while I was quiet. I wanted to be helpful and engage in the class while Dontae just wanted to antagonize me. Apparently Miss Battle saw us as one and the same: poor Black kids she stuck in the back of the classroom.

I will never forget when Miss Battle walked up to my desk and looked at the report I had made with red paper lining the white.

"I want to be a lawyer," I said to her.

"That will never happen," she told me with a cruel smirk.

The comment stunned me. It felt like time stood still, as my face turned hot with shame and surprise. I wondered who was watching and whether Dontae Eliot was taking this all in with a smug smile to taunt me later.

Why can't I be a lawyer? I didn't get to ask my question. My voice was gone for a few seconds, and Miss Battle stalked away, leaving me sitting quiet and withdrawn at my desk.

My teacher had apparently decided my potential—or lack of potential, as it was. And with a word, the woman in charge of educating and inspiring me landed a blow on me that was more effective than any kick from my desk mate.

But I took exception with her assessment and argued that I could be whatever I wanted to be. Soon my disagreement became shouting, and by the time I was screaming in an attempt to stand up for myself, I found myself shut down and sent to the principal's office. I was never able to argue my case before the court. My judge and jury made their decision before I even said a word.

Despite standing up for myself in the moment, for a long time after she spoke those words, I was convinced that Miss Battle was correct in her assumption about Michael Phillips. The weight of her disbelief hung heavily on me.

You carry the words heard during childhood with you throughout life. Sometimes it takes many years to realize where those words—and the messages behind them—came from.

"What is the quality of your intent?" Thurgood Marshall once asked. "Certain people have a way of saying things that shake us at the core. Even when the words do not seem harsh or offensive, the impact is shattering. What we could be experiencing is the intent behind the words. When we intend to do good, we do. When we intend to do harm, it happens. What each of us must come to realize is that our intent always comes through."

A compliment can carry you into a career you never might have imagined. Discouraging words can demoralize you and delay the dreams you once envisioned.

That day, Miss Battle's words shook me. In seconds I went from having the eagerness for self-discovery to having feelings of self-denial. Maybe she was right. After all, wasn't she the teacher?

I wondered for a long time how a teacher could say such a thing to a child. *Maybe,* I considered, *Miss Battle was speaking out of her own pain.* One day while thinking about this, I realized something.

Wait a second. She lived two blocks up the street from our home.

Miss Battle lived in the same place I came from. Just a few yards separated our worlds. Perhaps it was her world—no, *our* world—that caused her to think so little of me. Perhaps her expectations were shaped by old stereotypes. Perhaps she had just seen too much, had her hopes for one promising student or another dashed as year followed year. Was something wrong with her that day? Maybe she was just speaking out of fatigue or out of her institutional memory. The body has the uncanny ability to keep score. We carry our wins and losses through memories, accomplishments, failures, and hurts. Maybe Miss Battle couldn't believe in my dreams because she had lost faith in her *own* dreams years ago. Perhaps in some way we were both being affected by our community's diffidence and difficulties.

All of the above could have been the answer. I could not know her past or what she carried with her. But what is most likely, based on the stark reality of her vitriolic response, is this: Miss Battle had deep implicit and explicit biases. If our encounter was any evidence, she simply didn't believe in the children she taught. She didn't believe we were capable of great things.

Bias. As a kid, I didn't know what the terms *redlining* or *white flight* meant (even though they affected my neighborhood), nor had I ever heard of the Fair Housing Act of 1968. I couldn't have comprehended the systems that were in place and once backed by the US government that prevented Black men and women from buying homes in certain neighborhoods by denying them mortgages. It didn't matter that I lived in a community of individuals who woke up every day and worked just as hard as anybody else—men and women who paid their taxes and families who went to church. The people in my neighborhood were "as American as apple pie," even though they didn't have an equal slice. The only difference between them and the White families who lived a couple of blocks away was the distance. The only difference between Miss Battle's address and mine was the invisible red line that had been drawn by the biased hands of individuals that I would never meet. The disconcerting policy for housing created a gap within a few blocks that was enough to leave my community locked out of the American dream, with less wealth, more crime, and underfunded schools. Miss Battle's actions in the classroom were a microcosm of society. As it turns out, we both carried societal weight to school, the heavy cultural burdens that create a significant amount of trauma generationally.

I was in an education system where kids were, so to speak, incarcerated by their zip codes, and I felt it. Park Heights was an interesting place where you had mostly White families residing on one side and Black families on the other, buffered by the Pimlico Race Course. The invisible line determined where you went to school and where you could afford to live. If you were to drive just a few blocks up from where I lived on Rogers Avenue, you would pass the racetrack and come to The Suburban Club, an exclusive golf course and country club.

I used to ride my bike to the other side and stand outside the country club watching all these guys playing golf and wondering what it was like. Never once did I see someone who resembled me on the course hitting balls or driving a cart. A few *blocks* away from my neighborhood, it felt like an entirely different universe. That world of caddies and five irons felt totally out of reach for me. No matter how much I visualized being there, the awkward stares from the people

on the other side of the fence told me that I could only visit . . .
and reinforced the idea that my dreams were, somehow, invalid.

When dreams die, the human spirit dies. The greatest injustice that can be imposed on the human spirit is the termina-
tion of its ability to dream, and too often, this takes place
during our childhood.

The studies show that spending two years under an ineffective teacher demonstrably destroys a child's potential,
while two years under an effective teacher can create a scholar
and unlock genius. According to the Learning Policy Institute, there is "a positive link between teacher professional
development, teaching practices, and student outcomes." Simply, this is stating an obvious but profound truth: *how we
teach shapes how kids learn.*

On the surface, my experience with Miss Battle could
seem small and insignificant. It was my moment of encoun-
tering the low expectations of an ineffective teacher, someone
who had no passion to fan the spark in my eyes. Yet it underscores the severity of implicit and explicit bias, the stiffness of
structural inequality and inequity, and the generative nature
of disadvantage. Note that equality is not the same as equity.
Equity is tailored to the continuity of every child's purpose. It
means for any practice, program, decision, or action, the impact on all students is addressed. As the saying goes, equality

will give everyone a pair of shoes, but equity will give everyone a pair of shoes that fit. I don't know everything about Miss Battle or her inner motivations. But based on her attitude and actions, it sure seems that because I lived where I lived and looked how I looked, my teacher judged me callously and predetermined my life's outcome as easily as if she were changing channels on a television.

The opportunity to dream was not provided for me that day; instead, I was sent to the office for arguing with the teacher. The institution that was charged to prepare me for my dreams almost suspended me for articulating them.

In our society, the most important factor that impacts the educational future of children is where they happen to live. Unfortunately this factor—not related to merit, hard work, academic interest, or other more nuanced aspects of character—largely determines the opportunities children receive or never get to experience. Your zip code has inordinate power to dictate your educational future.

And it largely wields this influence through teachers— whose various levels of resources, training, and skill in their work often (but of course not always!) bear some relationship to the affluence of the school district. For schools like the one I attended, the same red lines that were drawn around the communities were also drawn around the teachers. It's about quality. The awful thing about redlining is that all property is innately valuable. However, the narrative is controlled by individuals who do not see a certain property or person as valuable. Even though only a few blocks separated me and Miss Battle, an invisible line stood between us that made her house more valuable than mine. When we provide schools with teachers who aren't quality, we do the same thing that we do with home values. President Barack Obama said, "From the moment students enter a school, the most important factor in their success is not the color of their skin or the income of their parents, it's the person standing at the front of the classroom." But if that person doesn't love and believe in the children she is teaching, then how can we have successful outcomes?

I believe every person has genius inside him. That of course can be demonstrated in different ways, through avenues like the arts, athletics, academics, or working with one's hands. I believe that the overwhelming majority of teachers who fight as hard as they can every day for the kids that they educate believe this as well. However, I'm not certain whether the overwhelming majority of educators today can admit to working in a system that is still inherently unequal. And if we're not willing to see the impact this has, how will we be able to find workable solutions together? With any problem, the first step to solving it is *naming* it.

The etymology of the word *educate* indicates that it means to "bring up, to train" and to "bring out, lead forth . . . with . . . nurture and support." So it is fair for us to ask whether our system of education is presently doing that. Yet as of the twenty-first century, the United States has largely designed a school system whose effects often do not look much like education. Ours is a compulsory system that is generally one-size-fits-all, widely divergent in quality based on place and affluence, and built on the premise of instilling conformity rather than cultivating creativity. As bad as that is, inherent in the idea of standardization is the reality that Black and Brown children have often not been fairly included in the concept of *all*. From the overt segregation of Jim Crow–era schools to the "softer" segregation that we usually see today, it is clear that the system is not working as its own ideals would demand. Speaking as a Black man, I recognize that we were not the individuals that the system seemed to care much about or intended to invest in. In policies such as residential assignment and practices such as not allowing kids to be tested for giftedness, the apparent belief (like Miss Battle held) of a hierarchy of human value is deeply imprinted in education.

Intelligence isn't learned; it's discerned. We are all born with unique genius. Every single person has her own unique set of talents and gifts and potentials. There is not a child who does not hold something precious with which to live a useful and beautiful life. This idea is evident in the instruction God gave to Adam and Eve: "Be fruitful." You cannot be fruitful unless you're "seed-full." The implication is that each of us holds huge potential. Each and every one of us has the seeds of genius—would we not need that to be fruitful? Of course. Potential doesn't need to be added to our lives; it needs to be cultivated. And with this incredible backdrop of the potential present in each and every child, here is the great tragedy: arguably, our system of education doesn't cultivate genius; instead, it anesthetizes it.

Our individual genius comes not from what we know but from how we disseminate and articulate the information we have accumulated and how we contribute by means of that to society. Our genius does not depend on education. But education can massively empower or suppress it.

For an example, let's look at two musicians of genius: Stevie Wonder and Miles Davis.

I had an old soul as a kid. My uncle had a basement full of albums from the '60s and '70s, mostly R&B, jazz, and funk, so I spent many hours listening to and loving those records. Stevie Wonder's *Songs in the Key of Life* is still one of my favorites. When you study both Stevie Wonder and Miles Davis, you see two respective geniuses who excelled in their craft as songwriters and performers. While they worked in different genres and produced very different music, their genius was rooted in everything they brought to their pieces— but it was also *cultivated* by a rich culture of the arts. Their souls came out in their songs because their inherent gifts were nurtured, trained, and supported. Miles's father was a prosperous dentist, while his mother was an accomplished keyboard player and violinist. His father gave him a trumpet at age thirteen, and by the time he was eighteen, Miles convinced his parents to send him to the Juilliard School in New York. Stevie sang in his church choir as a child and learned to play the piano, harmonica, and drums at a young age.

My Bruce Lee–kicking adversary in Miss Battle's class could have been Miles while I could have been Stevie. What if we had that type of school system where all kids could be confident in their imaginations? What if what we were good at was valued or, at the least, cultivated at school? Inopportunely, our system causes a significant number of individuals to lose confidence over time. As a result, before we become adults, many of us have not found our passions or purposes. We've been taught to believe that conventionality is the way to success. Dreaming impossible dreams isn't an option when you have to conform to mediocre standards. What if many of our educational problems today are not because we expect too much of our young people but because we expect too little? What if we began to see our schools not primarily as dispensaries of knowledge but as keys to unlock the inner genius of our students—by means of rigorous learning?

Education should drive us to our passions. When life brings detours, education should also provide some guardrails. The system that we have, in which teachers have to do their best to nurture, support, and bring out the latent potential of their students, doesn't support the teachers adequately either. In my opinion, teachers are champions. They do incredible things. They represent the second line of defense for the potential of our children. After parents they are this nation's greatest advocates for young people.

I was unfortunate enough to have the antithesis. Miss Battle looked at what I *didn't* appear to have, simply based on a superficial impression. She didn't bother trying to find out what I could offer. If a child knows what he's got, if his genius has been unearthed, he will pursue and go after it. But creating a system of deficiency that produces the sort of school I was in makes it too easy for a student to say, "Yeah, this isn't for me. I'm dropping out." Creating a system of deficiency causes students to live on the edges of those lines, making it easier for them to fall off. Kids who drop out have been asked to live life on the margins where there's no room, where they eventually ask, "Where's my life? What can I do? You never showed me."

"None of us got where we are solely by pulling ourselves up by our bootstraps," Thurgood Marshall said. "We got here because somebody—a parent, a teacher, an Ivy League crony or a few nuns—bent down and helped us pick up our boots."

The very person who was supposed to bend down and help me pick up my boots—or notice if I even had a pair of boots to pick up—crushed my hopes and dreams. I was six years old, and someone was telling me who I couldn't be. It felt like being punched in the face. With just a few cruel words, Miss Battle shut down my dreaming.

It would seem that the significant work of Thurgood Marshall to integrate schools and promote equity in education should have distanced me from the racial bias explicit in Miss Battle's expectations of my capacity and perhaps that of many other students. But time reflecting on this experience has allowed me to come to the discovery of this bitter truth: tragedy and silence often live on the same block.

My experience in first grade in the early 1980s was symptomatic of an educational reality that would later become a national emergency. I was in a declining school system where only about 5 percent of the student population was proficient in reading and math. For years this system would fail to educate students. The rapid decline in our school was perpetuated by a wider slippery slope of troubling social realities in our community. Safety and support deteriorated, and academic achievement got worse each year.

But the pinnacle of the problem in my school and community was a decline in care. Little by little, I began to see boarded-up houses and addicted people and unkempt lawns and closing businesses. The landscape of the community completely changed, and when people see something dwindling and deteriorating, they find it easier to trash it. As the community goes down, everything goes further downhill with it, especially the schools. Seeing that type of blight every day creates indifference. That same indifference was found in our education system.

When something you love begins to fall apart, it builds a certain level of indifference in you that makes you feel powerless, like it's never going to change. You develop an attitude of *Why bother?* You can take the boards off the doors and mow the lawns, but indifference doesn't allow that type of optimism.

In 1983, indifference seemed to sweep all over our country as a report stated that the greatest threat to national security was our inability to cultivate our collective brilliance. We'd become used to seeing individuals suffer. In the same way my community was deteriorating, so was the country. This tidal wave of indifference prompted the famous report *A Nation at Risk,* released by the National Commission on Excellence in Education in April 1983. The commission was created by then US education secretary Terrel Bell, and the report took eighteen months to complete. The summary was ominous instead of optimistic, with warnings such as "The educational foundations of our society are presently being eroded by a rising tide of mediocrity that threatens our very future as a Nation and as a people." The report, addressed as an "open letter" to all Americans, declared the public school system was in "desperate" need of improvement.

In first grade, I sat in a classroom seat dealing firsthand with the mediocrity and bias that were threatening the future of the nation, but I wonder if the purpose and potential of a Black boy were a part of that risk assessment. My elementary school did not believe I had much to offer.

I've never liked sitting still. I also like to learn visually. My way of connecting with material I'm learning is to paint pictures in my head of the concepts being taught and then to look for aspects of them in my surroundings—to connect where I am with what we're talking about. But my visual-spatial learning style was not conducive to the regimented confines of my teachers' classrooms. By third grade one of my teachers wanted me to be tested for special needs. My mother refused, saying that if they wanted to test me, I needed to be tested for being gifted and talented, not for special needs. Looking back now, I think I just had BOOMM syndrome. (I was *bored out of my mind*.) By fourth grade? Yet *another* teacher told me that I would end up in jail . . . just because I couldn't sit still in my seat.

Were we not being cared for because we were Black and because of where we lived? Was this equal education? Did the much-lauded *Brown v. Board of Education* case have an unintended impact on the most vulnerable communities?

Despite the Supreme Court's landmark decision in *Brown v. Board of Education* over sixty-five years ago, the arguments about racial inequalities in the nation's educational system persist today. Residential assignment continues to drive discrepancies in resources between schools in affluent and disadvantaged communities. Segregation still haunts the halls of our schools not just by race but also by income. In 2019, the *New York Times* wrote that "more than half of the nation's schoolchildren are in racially concentrated districts, where over 75 percent of students are either white or non-white." A later article stated, "The nexus of racial and economic segregation has intensified educational gaps between rich and poor students, and between White students and students of color." Looking through the lens of equity, we see that non-White schools receive $23 billion less in funding even though they serve the same number of students.

While we applaud what we gained in the *Brown* case—equal access—we cannot either ignore the equity that we lost or deny that there is some equity we never had. The rich and culturally competent pedagogy of Black educators was decimated by the *Brown v. Board* decision, which split the ends of the unequal educational rope that many Black and Brown children held on to.

Brown had the tragic effect of triggering the expulsion, demotion, or involuntary retirement of a variety of highly qualified Black educators who served in Black-only schools. There was no effective plan to value or adequately preserve their excellence or expertise after integration. "After the decision, tens of thousands of black teachers and principals lost their jobs as white superintendents began to integrate schools but balked at putting black educators in positions of authority over white teachers or students." This was an unintended and disastrous result of the *Brown* decision, especially in the South. Arguably, the continued shortage of Black teachers in American education today is *still* linked to the long-term effects of the *Brown v. Board of Education* ruling.

And is this a loss? Absolutely. Besides the anecdotal evidence—the power of having a teacher who looks like you and understands many of the realities that you experience—"a growing body of research has found that black students benefit from having a black teacher, both academically and socially." A 2017 Johns Hopkins study found that "low-income black students who have at least one black teacher in elementary school are significantly more likely to graduate high school and consider attending college." Unfortunately, my first Black instructor came when I was in middle school.

Black children who have Black teachers are "less likely to be suspended, expelled, or placed in detention," and they are more likely to be accepted in gifted-education classes. Johns Hopkins research from 2016 also shows that Black instructors' expectations for Black students are higher than those of White instructors. The silencing of Black educational voices created the disciplinary trenches that would come to feed the school-to-prison pipeline.

Behind every piece of data is an individual destiny.

Have you ever paused to think of the impact that statistics like these have—not only on minority communities but also on our nation and culture? Think of the lost years, the squandered potential, the lives ruined because our system is out of balance and unfairly skewed so that it does not represent its students. What have we all lost in this often-ignored pattern of tragedy?

Miss Battle sent me to the office for disciplinary reasons

more often than she gave us homework. If I asked a question without raising my hand, I was sent to the office. If I said I didn't understand what she was talking about, I was sent to the office. If I decided to go to the bathroom because I couldn't hold it, I was sent to the office and suspended for it.

This is considered exclusionary discipline, which is any kind of school discipline "that removes or excludes a student from his or her usual educational setting," and it is without question a discriminatory practice. It pushes children out of school and into the criminal justice system with no intention or way of restoring them to a learning environment, leaving most entangled in the conditions of punitive justice. A report by the American Psychological Association Services stated that "disparities in the use of exclusionary discipline can lead to a school-to-prison pipeline for some of the most vulnerable members of our society."

Have you ever wondered how a bright, hardworking kid could go from school to the streets and from the streets to a prison cell? It is a question we should be asking ourselves every day. *How?* People will offer all sorts of answers. But they will ignore the big one behind them all: *us.* We are how, through inaction and inequity as a culture. All the children are not well.

The only way to untangle this systemic Gordian knot of inequity and exclusion is to cut through it. We have to deal with race, trauma, and memory in education if we are going to uncouple our system from injustice. "Empirical and qualitative evidence . . . show that children thrive academically, behaviorally, and socially when they are part of inclusive and supportive school communities and have strong relationships with their teachers." For that to happen, the gap in teacher diversity has to close. Today approximately 79 percent of public school teachers are White, 9.3 percent are Hispanic, 7 percent are Black, and 2 percent are Asian. In the meantime, "slightly more than half of public school students are nonwhite."

When I was in school, I found myself fighting not to be pushed into the social chasm that bias creates. Most days I stood on the edge of that chasm in silence as I entered the classroom, my stomach tied in knots, hoping that one day I wouldn't feel this way.

This was the beginning of my journey through school to the streets, and I wondered how things would turn out.

I wondered if I could ever escape the feeling of inadequacy.

I wondered, thinking of the words of the old gospel hymn, how my soul would make it over.

CHAPTER TWO

The Predator and
the Prey

It's like a jungle sometimes
It makes me wonder how I keep from goin' under
—GRANDMASTER FLASH and the FURIOUS FIVE

Sometimes the greatest foes in the fight to help kids succeed in life are simply the forces that exist in their environment. Lurking, restless, and waiting in the shadows. Too
many dark things to overcome.

Right up the street from my elementary school, in the opposite direction of my house, was a notorious apartment
complex. We were always warned to stay away from that
place. "Don't go up there," my parents often told me. But one
of the spots that made my neighborhood *fun* was in the same
area, and we all loved going there to hang out. The corner
store was a community hub (with video games inside!), a

place to buy penny candy and chicken boxes. Four pieces of fried chicken wings, french fries, and a dinner roll in a little white box for five bucks were pure *joy*. If you had an extra dollar, you could get one hundred pieces of assorted candy; Squirrel Nut Chews were my favorites. These little corner stores were ubiquitous in Baltimore and usually run by families who did not ethnically or racially resemble my own.

"Come straight home after school," my mother said. "Do *not* go to the corner store."

She knew that trouble lived in close proximity to pain, but what pain was she trying to keep me from? I didn't really know. Her assumption was that you can be safe living on the periphery of other people's problems. But telling me not to go to the store was like a lioness telling a young cub not to go to the watering hole, knowing what else is in the jungle. To the cub, the jungle is the jungle. To me, my neighborhood was my neighborhood. The danger she wisely feared was cloaked by the indescribable beauty that was in my community. Everyone went to that store. Whether it was good or bad, it was ours. It was the one place you could go to see some joy in the midst of pain. My mother's caveat wasn't my concern; my friends were. And my friends went to the store.

A sense of belonging tends to make us ignore the wisdom that knows about the unseen dangers around us. Beneath the canopy of our concrete jungle was a darkness that had the power to pull us down into the urban quicksand. My mother didn't want me to step into the kind of situations where no matter what you do, things get only worse. Interacting more and more with the fringe area of my neighborhood was not only dangerous, but it also could possibly put the danger in a person.

The culture that surrounded us was magnificent and violent. I know that sounds contradictory. But my neighborhood was much like the color purple. When you see purple, you think of royalty and beauty, richness. But the bruises that we get on our bodies are purple also. Over time, the beauty of my neighborhood shifted from the richness of real community fabric to the purple of a bruise. People hurt. People were hurt. People continued to be diminished as the bruises they suffered overwhelmed them, making the majority of hearts in our neighborhood hard and insensitive to the difficulties of life. Callousness to painful situations became the norm. As years brought more pain, it became far harder to feel shocked by any violence. Hard times were our way of life. My mother knew that some of the turmoil in our community was not normal, but before I could fully understand why that was true, I came to accept everything that came with my community.

By the tender age of eight, I was accustomed to seeing strangers, friends, neighbors, and even relatives getting high. At that age I didn't understand addiction or the generational impact addiction has. The corner store was where all the *fun* people were, but right across the street was where all the *ill* people were. It took some time for me to know the difference between an addict and an adult.

I didn't even fully comprehend what I was doing when I helped sell drugs for the first time. I wasn't even a teenager. Near the store, a neighborhood guy on the corner waved me over and asked for a favor. "Hey, little man. Why don't you take this over there for me and I'll get you something to eat from the store."

"Sure." I thought this was a great idea. Raymond handed me a little brown bag. I brought it over to another guy, who gave me some cash, which I then carried back to Raymond. What did I know? Little lions don't know that crocodiles generally don't hunt outside the water. They wait for their prey to come to the edge.

It was the mid-'80s, and Baltimore, like many other big cities, was starting to change. There was a new drug. The illegal drug market had been dominated by heroin, but crack cocaine began to surge into major cities, producing what would become the "crack epidemic" that lasted into the mid-'90s. Crack was like a gold rush in the hood. It was potent and could be easily smoked. It was simple to produce, affordable on the streets, and highly profitable for dealers.

Crack was the perfect drug for the predator-prey system that marginalized communities have endured for generations. The political response to combat the epidemic of crack and the crime that followed was a continuation of the War on Drugs. President Nixon's administration had initiated this concept with policies to target major importers and traffickers of illegal drugs in the 1970s. Yet instead of targeting those groups and offering more educational programs as well as drug treatment opportunities, legislators under Nixon and later under President Reagan decided to target street-level users and dealers. Federal funding was split, with 70 percent of it going toward law enforcement and 30 percent toward programming such as the famous Just Say No campaign. Oddly, policymakers refused to consider a treatment-on-demand approach despite knowing that tens of thousands wanted access to treatment. Penalizing rather than restoring users was, seemingly, preferable to those in power. With mandatory minimum sentences ranging from one year to life imprisonment, drug users, the vast majority of whom simply needed help, were incarcerated for their illness, and penalties for repeat offenders were even harsher. War on Drugs? Maybe the term was apt. Like most wars, it seemed to sure have a lot of collateral damage.

We did not understand the true nature of the crisis, and as a society we often overreact to social issues that we do not understand. "During the 1980s, Congress created the Sentencing Commission, an appointed panel that established strict sentencing guidelines" and (predictably) expanded drug-related penalties. The Sentencing Reform Act of 1984, which created the commission, "also eliminated parole and required all inmates to serve at least 85 percent of their sentences behind bars before becoming eligible for release." All of these punitive measures failed to address the most basic questions of why the epidemic was happening in the first place and what kinds of response would help restore vulnerable people and communities instead of destroying them.

The collateral damage from the policies enacted by the War on Drugs would create a deficit of hope in Black and Brown communities across the country and place an avoidable burden on the nation for years to come. The casualties from this war were too many to count. Sometimes it felt like we were all driving down a hopeless highway, with a foot on the gas, no brakes, and no off-ramps.

I was ten years old when I saw my first murder. I had grown used to the typical hood drama—someone getting chased down the street over a small beef or some joker getting run off the block by guys with baseball bats over some foolishness like talking to the wrong girl. But that day my life changed forever.

As I was coming out of the corner store, the joy that I normally experienced instantly turned to pain. First I saw Raymond on the corner like always; then I noticed a man stepping out in front of him with a shotgun. Raymond was shot and killed right in front of me. Everyone else scrambled and ran. I froze. My ten-year-old brain could not comprehend what had just happened. Not at first. Then I dropped everything and ran too. I went straight for home, sprinting as fast as I could down the sidewalks and through the alley into my house.

I was in my room crying when my mother opened the door.

"What's wrong, Michael?"

"They shot Raymond," I replied. The words seemed so hollow. They couldn't really contain what I had seen.

She walked over to my bed. It creaked quietly as she sat beside me. It was obvious she was not shocked, but she was sorry. In a soft and assured tone, she began to tell me about the world outside and how things were. I would have to learn fast if I was going to make it.

"You know, Raymond wasn't a good guy . . ." Mom's words hung in the air. "But he didn't deserve to die like that," she continued.

"He was always good to *me*," I said, wiping tears from my face.

What would make people risk their lives by standing on corners and selling drugs every day knowing that if it went bad, the consequences would be jail time or death? Is it bad character or poor decision-making? Is it just financial incentive? Most people would attribute it to one of those options. But be careful anytime you find an easy answer to a complicated issue. Personal responsibility is where the buck stops in our culture—but the reasons why people do what they do never come easily. There are always multiple underlying factors in the choices we make. Beneath each personal choice is a sea of unchosen influences, experiences, and factors that shape our circumstances and our characters. When a dangerous wave rises from that sea and crushes some good thing, who is responsible? Yes, we all have choices. But is the way we make them ever simple?

What we often overlook, what seems to evade us when we try to understand, is the limited options some people have based on their conditions. Living in disinvested communities; attending poor schools; pushing against cultural norms of skepticism, apathy, or hostility; and maybe not even having the opportunities to make a living wage are issues we often choose not to calculate into our judgments of others—especially if we have not experienced these ourselves. Some people have harder decisions to make, but we tend to judge one another based on the curated images those who do not live in similar circumstances give us while we excuse similar behavior from the people we identify with the most.

Noted criminologist Alfred Blumstein explained it this way: In the 1970s drug use was "principally a white phenomenon" among affluent to middle-income individuals. Blumstein reported in a 1992 presidential address to the American Society of Criminology that from the late 1960s to the early 1980s, "white arrest rates for juvenile drug offenses were higher than those for black juveniles," but both rates dropped dramatically after 1974. White arrest rates continued to fall into the early 1980s, but Black arrest rates shot up four to five times higher and continued at that rate well into the 1990s. The reason for this is what Blumstein called the "our kids, their kids" explanation. Simply put, when White kids do drugs, efforts are made to decriminalize usage, but when minorities do drugs, efforts are made to criminalize the act. From 1980 to 1993, the prison population in America tripled.

Being male and Black means confronting "on a daily basis, a deeply held racism that exists in every social institution." Black males have fared obstinately worse than any other demographic group in America—with the arguable exception of male Indigenous Americans. The life outcomes for Black males are bleak in just about every domain. From education to low-paying employment, from life expectancy to incarceration, you will find us ranking at the bottom or top, respectively. Black men make up the largest share of the prison population in America. As a group we are more likely to die prematurely than any other demographic. According to the Bureau of Labor Statistics, Black men have the highest unemployment rate in the country, and that doesn't include men who are incarcerated or the ones not looking for work. The exhaustive list of disadvantages goes on and on.

None of these data are the result of bad character or poor choices. They are the "direct result of centuries of vilification and pernicious narratives" that depicted African American males as less than human. The myth of the aggressive African American man has a long history in the United States. The stereotypes that focused "on labeling blacks, particularly black males as 'brutes' and 'savage-like,' criminal, lewd, hypersexual, or predatory" have not significantly diminished in our society. And these harmful stereotypes shape the lives of those they most affect.

Black males in our culture are "guilty" of being Black males until they can prove their "innocence"—by rising above the false narratives and consistent hurdles that they face. It's no wonder, then, that some men like Raymond decide to become invisible because they discover over time that they are the most vulnerable. Being raised in segregated neighborhoods, either in concentrated poverty or in close proximity to it, and being cut off from economic opportunity will make just about anyone take the risk to create his own opportunity.

Raymond wasn't a predator. He was prey.

The Cinderella Shoe Store was where you would go to see royalty. Everybody stood outside this sneaker store, and most of them were the neighborhood drug dealers. They always wore fresh gear, blinged out with gold chains, and leaned on their tinted Cressidas and Jeeps with booming sound systems. These young men were invisible to society, but they were kings in my neighborhood. Raymond was one of them. In most of my interactions with him, he would say to me, "I got to do what I got to do, but you, little man, don't have to do what I do."

Raymond was twenty years old, a high school dropout with a two-year-old daughter. Standing on that corner for him was about survival. Historically, sixteen- to eighteen-year-olds who drop out of school have the most trouble in our society. However, many eighteen- to twenty-four-year-old Black males who graduated from high school but are not enrolled in any sort of postsecondary schooling remain out of work, and the ones who are employed make too little to support themselves and their families. Unemployment and low income have been the norm for Black males for generations, and the cycles have been extremely challenging to break.

It's hard to become what you never see.

It's even harder when society tells you that you have no value. I could count on one hand how many Black male professionals I saw growing up, and I probably wouldn't need to use all five fingers. Other than at church, I never saw anybody prominent from my community that looked like me. Dropping out of school was the norm, and graduating high school and going to college were the exception.

Exposure is everything.

The lack of exposure to possibility creates small dreams, and when the ground you're supposed to stand on becomes the roof over you, options become limited. You feel trapped. I can see how the guys on the corner found it easy to say, *I'll risk my life for this little bit of reward of hood prestige because I can't be anything else in the world.* I can see how easy it is to fall into that trap and lose your life.

You gravitate toward what is valued, and in my environment, that was either the corner or sports. I thought I would end up like Raymond if I chose the corner. Thankfully, my father exposed me to a different way of life.

At the same time the crack epidemic was peaking, the U.S. Department of Housing and Urban Development (HUD) was studying the effect "place" had on one's social mobility. One study was Moving to Opportunity (MTO). Several thousand families living in the most economically challenged public-housing locations in the country were given the opportunity through a lottery to relocate to a lower-poverty area using a housing voucher. This study gave us a very visible picture of the impact neighborhoods have on families, as well as the effects of physical environment on both adults and their children.

Over 4,600 families from high-poverty areas in Baltimore, Chicago, Boston, New York, and Los Angeles participated in this study, and data on them was tracked through 2010. When finally distilled and analyzed, the data showed that the lives of children under the age of thirteen improved after they moved to a better neighborhood. They ended up earning about 31 percent more income as adults, and a higher percentage ended up going to college. The reason is not because they were living in better houses or had better neighbors. It's the quality of education they received and the level of positive exposure that came with it.

When kids begin to learn at a younger age, they pick up the skills and tools to stay interested and to grow. The stronger the educational opportunities, the more likely the children will experience positive life outcomes as they transition to adulthood.

Changing one's location is just one step, and for older children and adults, that's not always the antidote. The key lies in the schools. Nelson Mandela understood this when he said, "Education is the most powerful weapon we can use to change the world."

My first time at Memorial Stadium to see a Baltimore Orioles game was full of anticipation and excitement. I was so excited to see my Eddie Murray. The future Baseball Hall of Famer nicknamed "Steady Eddie" played first baseman for the Orioles from 1977 to 1988, then went on to play for the Los Angeles Dodgers, the New York Mets, and the Cleveland

Indians. Murray was a superstar, and watching him and the Orioles made me become enamored with the sport. It helped that the Orioles won their third World Series in 1983.

At the time, baseball wasn't something cherished in my neighborhood, but my neighbor and his family were huge baseball fans. Andre was the kid that had everything; he had the best glove, the best bat, the best bike. We were close friends and really competitive. If he jumped five trash cans, then I was going to jump ten. Andre helped inspire my love of baseball. When I saw Eddie Murray on television in commercials and interviews, I thought to myself, *Oh, I can do that!* I knew I was fast, so I asked my father to buy me a glove and decided to start playing baseball.

The first time a ball got into my glove, I knew sports and not education would be my ticket out of my neighborhood.

The world around me was not conducive to the success I saw on television, though. No matter how much I tried to emulate it, the treatment I received from society wasn't the same. I just wanted people to be nice to me like they were to Eddie Murray and other Black male sports figures. The more I noticed the differences in treatment, the more I depended on my father to help me make sense of why the world hated Black men but loved Black athletes. My father would often listen to the other young men at his church who shared their confusion at how they were perceived in the world. They would say things like "You have no idea what it's like dealing with what I'm dealing with and living where I'm living and struggling how I'm struggling and hoping how I'm hoping and trying how I'm trying. You have no idea."

That's when my dad would say to them, "I know exactly how you feel." What became clear to me, hearing my father say those words, is that most Black men have to fight off the pallbearers of their potential and the predators of their purpose.

The complexity of our social Serengeti makes it virtually impossible for anyone on the outside looking in to be able to understand and empathize, let alone sympathize, with somebody she has no reference to. Those on the outside see Black-on-Black crime—which is not a thing. We see pain in proximity to pain. The world watches from a limited perspective and easily discounts the experience of Black males who fight to survive in segregated communities.

My community needed triage, not criticism.

Condemnation of vulnerable communities will not change them, especially when we disparage the *what* without knowing the *why*. The collective damage of an environment full of violence and absent of validation perpetuates itself. There is a long-established link between exposure to violence and juvenile delinquency. To put it another way, victimized individuals become more violent over time or, better yet, "violence breeds violence." Friends I had at a young age, guys I played with in the alleyway and saw regularly going to the store or at school, changed rapidly. Year by year as we got older, I watched them slowly become more desperate and more aggressive for the sake of survival. When one of us got picked off and we saw the pallbearers come, you could see a switch go off in our heads that suggested we would strike first to avoid becoming casualties. Each year, I lost somebody or saw a person's trajectory change. It was as if we were all being sifted like wheat but we were only the chaff. Over the edge my friends went, pulled into darkness and fighting to find their way out—living in fear and turning to aggression to cope with the horrible things that can be remedied only by collateral hope.

It was Victor Hugo who wrote, "There is nothing like a dream to create the future." But what do you do with dreams that are covered by the dust of too many disappointments? How do you look forward to a future that's concealed by the ashes of departed heroes? You don't feel safe enough to dream anymore, and you don't see many paths to pursue. Think of what this robs from a young person!

In adversity, often one key to survival is to not allow your mind to become ensnared by the environment in which you've been brought up. Another key is to give your pain a voice. You must let the agony pass *through* you instead of storing it up in your heart, giving you little chance of escape. Often this looks like replacing negative supports of your self-esteem that you've been relying on with more positive ones, getting used to the idea that there is *more* for you outside whatever small, hurtful place you're in.

As a boy, my neighborhood was an urban underbrush. Though it was dangerous, it also provided some cover for many of us. We needed that. Why? Because the unidimensional systems that awaited us were far more menacing predators than the ones the world liked to depict. The criminal justice system, the education system—they had only one dimension. The model didn't fit the moment. Take Raymond, for example. He wasn't as much of a predator as he was a prey. The social systems that were designed to foster opportunity weren't given to Black men for generations. Even if you wanted to be a scientist or if you had the proclivity to be an engineer or something like that, there have been times in our country's history when you never got those opportunities.

The Pullman porters are an obvious example.

Right after the Civil War, a businessman from Chicago named George Pullman hired thousands of Black men to work on his railroad sleeping cars serving White passengers. These porters, many of whom were recently freed slaves, were paid little and overworked. George Pullman realized these men knew how to cater to customers, and he claimed to give them an opportunity, but all he wanted was to keep them locked into an expectation.

Being a porter meant working endless hours with little or no sleep and no time off. Porters shined shoes and served food and carried baggage and served at the beck and call of the passengers. Working for the Pullman Palace Car Company was desirable for Blacks, yet once in that position, they couldn't advance. The position came with the recognition that said, *This is it for you.*

Men like Raymond refused to simply be Pullman porters carrying other people's bags so they could get to their destinations. What about Raymond's destination? Society was asking him to carry the baggage of other people's biases and hatred and low expectations, but Raymond refused to be bound by this box. He was an entrepreneur and creator, so he went where there were opportunities for this. And the only place was in the underworld.

In some strange way, Raymond and my neighborhood were harbingers for my optimism because they rejected the one dimensional expectations we've built. Rather, I saw Black men doing well even though they were doing illegal things.

My conflict arose from the fact that what I was being taught at home was at odds with my neighborhood. I loved the environment—I wasn't so much trying to get out of it as allowing it to safely protect me from a scary world. Even though it had scary parts, my neighborhood environment didn't cause me to cast my ambitions aside.

But my father would say to me, "Yes, people can overcome their environment, but should they have to?" He challenged me to not allow people to devalue who I was or where

I lived. He taught me that self-pity cannot make you safe; it makes you believe that you'll always be its prey. My dad would read poems to me from authors like D. H. Lawrence, whose words still stay with me:

I never saw a wild thing
sorry for itself.

And we would discuss the truth and beauty of those words. Dad showed me that no one will pity you, not even when you hear the following words inside you: *You are nothing and never will be anything. The street is the only place you belong. There is no way out.* These messages, internalized because of a hard culture, were not the end of the story. At least, they didn't have to be.

My father made sure, despite the limited view for opportunity, that *possibility* remained in my mind. Something bigger, something better was somewhere out there beyond the fray. He admonished me to press past the boundary—when I did, I would find some opportunity as vast as the Atlantic. The water would be endless, a few islands of excellence in the distance. I began to look to those islands. They stood out.

My dad had enough faith for both of us. Prompted by these conversations with my father, I began to ponder, *Who could be my hero? Whom could I model my life after?* I would rather be an island of excellence floating out there somewhere than be more water in the sea of mediocrity. Hearing that you are different than you've been told inspires a fight in you to *live*. My social structure did not have to be my identity.

"Nobody else has your fingerprint, Michael," my dad would say. "Nobody else has your purpose."

My dad.

My hero.

CHAPTER THREE

How Are the Children?

No role models and I'm here right now.

—J. Cole

The traditional culture of the Maasai people is a wealth of
wisdom, melding a powerful fighting spirit with a nur-
turing domesticity that values the family and village life.
Their customary warriors' greeting *"Kasserian Ingera"* means
"How are the children?" It reflects "the high value that the
Maasai always put on their children's well-being." *All* warriors, even those men without children, respond with the old,
familiar reply of *"Sapati Ingera"*: "All the children are well."

The meaning of the exchange is to stress, every time they
meet, that in their culture they fight on behalf of their young,
to protect the most vulnerable. The intact Maasai culture

models this priority in front of those very children—to show what responsibility and duty are in the tribe and to ensure that the next generation doesn't lose sight of its obligations to the unborn generation that will follow. "All the children are well" indicates that life is valuable and that the future matters. It makes certain that everyday hardships of survival do not distract or prevent them from the priority of a healthy culture: caring well for their children.

All the children are well. Let those words sit. Is this our culture? No. Though there is no question that many parents shape their lives around their children (often with mixed results), where is the collective concern not just for "my kids" but for "*our* kids"? What would happen if our society adopted that beautiful value? What would happen if instead of "How are you?" we heard "How are the children?" a dozen times a day, passing it on to one another? I bet it would affect everything, even if slowly. Because we would quickly see that to give the expected reply in truth, we would have to either lie or get to the hard work. *All the children are well.*

There was a time in our communities when we protected, cultivated, and championed the potential of our children. It's debatable whether we still do, but the social and educational conclusions of multiple generations who have fallen into the gaps of inequity would probably win the argument. As controversial as this sounds, historically, communities of color were producing better outcomes for their children despite operating under "separate but equal" constraints. Don't get me wrong—segregation was demonic. But at least it brought with it a better education. Speaking as a Black man, I realize our elders understood that although we were cut off from opportunity in America, our ability was not. In the years of Jim Crow, a pro-academic tidal wave washed high on the hopeful shores of Black America, carrying good things in the surf.

In former slaveholding states, Black Americans saw education as a critical step toward gaining liberty and stability during the Reconstruction period. As a result, they discovered ways to learn amid the many impediments put in their paths by poverty and racism. For them, education was the way to uplift their communities and transform generations after enduring the intergenerational trauma of slavery. Our elders believed that the entire village needed to engage to ensure that children were educated, giving them their best chance toward social mobility and future success.

A remarkable model of this very idea existed in the most unlikely place at the most unlikely time. The Lincoln School in Marion, Alabama, was incorporated two years after the Civil War by nine ex-slaves. It was noted "for graduating a high proportion of students who went on to attain advanced degrees, a remarkable achievement . . . for a segregated high school." The entire village, not just the parents of students, pooled their resources around the school and their children with the intent of exposing them to professional models and individuals who looked like them and had accomplished phenomenal things. Coretta Scott King was only one of the many notable individuals who graduated from Lincoln. Doctors, lawyers, and PhDs came out of that environment. The Lincoln School operated for 103 years until it shut down due to state integration policies. African proverb or not, the old adage "It takes a village to raise a child" rings true.

If history and other cultural models prove that we can create healthy social and educational environments for our children, then why do we have such a stark contrast today? Could it be that our "village" is not well? Could it be that the constant struggles of the majority of society living in survival mode make cohesive community efforts impossible? If it takes a village to raise a child, then it takes a community to sustain the village. The incontrovertible proof that our village is not healthy is the lack of our children's well-being and the inability of adults to create a culture that will shift the outcomes from what we Christians might call generational curses to generational blessings.

Almost one in seven children in the US lives in poverty. That's approximately 10.5 million kids, or 14.4 percent—a rate one and a half times higher than adults. Approximately *71 percent* of children living in poverty are children of color. Until COVID-19 restrictions forced a shift to remote learning, school shootings were occurring more frequently every year, and daily gun violence continues to be a never-ending epidemic. Our juvenile justice system has tried kids as young as thirteen years old as adults.

Stop. Think about this. How have we allowed ourselves to become this way? How is America, for all her wealth and power, so put to shame by the Maasai, half a world away? How have we become content to live detached from the commitment we made as a society to pool our resources for the benefit of our children? How have we become so numb toward kids living in dangerous environments like the one I grew up in? *How?*

If we honestly contemplated these questions and reflected on why it's so difficult to end systemic issues like these, we would discover that as a society we are still hurting from the deep emotional wounds of historical trauma and the scars of deeply painful experiences as individuals and as groups.

Think about it this way. We all have bodies, right? And millions of us struggle against the pain of repetitive strain injuries every day. Carpal tunnel syndrome is a well-known example. One part of the body—the wrist—is forced to repeat an unnatural motion over and over to the point of fatigue. This happens until the nerves become permanently damaged and the pain becomes constant. In fact, these bodily injuries are called cumulative trauma disorders.

For many of us, racial trauma is a cumulative trauma too. People of color find ourselves sustaining emotional injury after emotional injury. Some of these seem very significant. Some of them may seem very small. But they all demand a response, a "motion." We repetitively force ourselves into unnatural positions (socially, personally, etc.) to try to protect ourselves from injury, but the hits just keep coming. Eventually the damage causes constant, undeniable pain in our minds and our hearts. The pain is soul deep.

Racial inequity and inequality are not only in our everyday environment but also in the body of our society. Many institutions in our communities and our culture contribute to the societal trauma and ensuing negative outcomes. This has been occurring generationally. For many of us, a painful racial history is not just our past. It is also our present.

This collective trauma has been transmitted across generations. Many of the negative dynamics that we see in play today are responses to societal trauma. From narcotic numbing to gang or domestic violence, from workaholism and success addiction to vocational apathy or trouble, we each respond *individually* to *community* legacies of pain. The unthinkable and the unexplainable that could not be contained in past generations have been passed along to us. This is the "paradox of survivorship," as one researcher puts it. Parents verbalize fear-based survival messages and pass them along to their children and grandchildren. Ideas like "Don't ask for help" or "It's dangerous out there—those people are trouble" become inherited messages that may have initially helped the oppressed stay safe. But over time, thoughts like those begin to cause the very damage they had hoped to prevent.

The consequences of transgenerational transmission are not just psychological. They are also parental, social, cultural, physiological, and likely even genetic. Without strong, healthy role models for the next generation (such as the dignified Maasai warriors walking among the children of the village), the agency to heal gets lost in the transmission. With each passing generation we begin to attempt to solve systemic issues by focusing on individual solutions. The stress is not just in the hand; it's in the whole body. The trauma-informed question we ought to be asking of each other, then, is not "What's wrong with us?" but "What happened to us?"

It takes a village to raise a child. But my village was not well. As I continued my childhood journey, the stress of being miseducated, living in a toxic environment, and not having the necessary role models was accumulating. It would impact me deeply when I became a teenager. After all, if it's hard to be what you don't see, then it's very easy to become what you do see.

One day, while driving with my dad on his way to work, we saw two little boys playing cops and robbers on the corner. One boy stood on the wall while the other patted him down and pretended he had found drugs on him. They couldn't have been much more than five. They were already acting out a drama that they had seen play out around them time and again. That was their model. That's what they consistently saw in their village.

My father, Richard Phillips, was a pastor. But like many preachers, that wasn't the whole story. He also had a full-time job driving a truck. He had an aversion to laziness and was allergic to quitting. He got up every day and did what he had to do without complaint and despite real struggle. Regardless of adversity, he modeled excellence for us.

"You got to know that you know that you know that you *know*." Out of the many things my father taught me, this truth was one of the most important. My dad showed me how to see—and reach—beyond my neighborhood. A village is not your neighborhood. It's more like a homestead of sorts, the surrounding network around your home. A real village extends beyond the boundaries of your neighborhood, a web of relationships much more complex than street names or strip malls.

On Dad's day runs, the normal route was from Baltimore to New York, but every now and then he'd go to Vermont or even up into Canada. When he took me with him, seeing each city and passing each state line exposed me to more possibilities and it lifted the cap off my imagination. A place like Niagara Falls blew my mind. By taking me to locations far away from Baltimore, my dad was encouraging me to imagine more. The city limits didn't have to be *my* limits. My father had a special grace—he embodied his faith. He believed in determination, no matter how improbable the mission might seem. Whenever I said I wanted to do something, his first response was to say, "Nothing is impossible for them that believe."

Even when he was making his runs with an eighteen-wheeler, my dad would talk with me about everything he wanted to accomplish. Which brings us back to the statement he'd make when he turned to me, eyes flashing between my face and the road: "You got to know that you know that you know that you *know*."

This was his funny way of saying a simple truth: no one is going to care as much about your vision as you do. People just won't. They can't, not really. And this was my father transmitting to me the same confidence he carried. No matter what, you have to *know* you know.

"You're going to get detractors confronting you about what you want to accomplish and do, so you have to know that you know that you know that you know, because no one else is going to know that for you."

Knowing what you can become is a sanctuary for your soul. Having someone to guide you along the way frees you from the concern of making it. My parents provided both for me. They were my examples.

Models are more powerful than mentors, and my parents were my models.

My dad was a phenomenal athlete. I'll never forget watching him play a pickup game in "Dru Hill" Park. He was an exceptional basketball player, a big guy standing six feet, four inches tall and built like a linebacker. A man's man. He had those snatching hands—the ones that could grab you no matter what church pew, city block, or park bench you were on. When he walked into a room, you knew that this was somebody who commanded respect. He looked mean, but the truth was that he was the most loving person you ever wanted to talk to. When I saw him school one of the biggest guys I'd ever seen on a basketball court at the time, a six-foot-nine behemoth, it was like watching a big David take down an enormous Goliath. Step back, fadeaway . . . *Swoosh!*

When he preached, hell stood at attention. When he sang and played the organ, heaven came down. Most impressive of all was his generosity. A lot of the guys around him were men with all types of struggles and addictions. It amazed me that a man could be so purposeful that he didn't have any time to be preoccupied with his own pain but used it to put others first.

My father would often pray in the mornings, and sometimes I would spy on him. He always passed by my bedroom door on the way downstairs. Since my room was next to the stairs, I would get up and sneak halfway down. I would sit on the steps and watch him in the living room praying. I wanted to get a glimpse of what this looked like, with the hope that one day I could bring heaven down like he did. Maybe I could make hell stand at attention, too, someday. Dad was my baseline. My model.

My mother, Sandra Phillips, encouraged me in her own ways. My sisters called her the Black Martha Stewart, and anyone with ears knew she was Patti LaBelle's vocal twin. Though we were not materially wealthy, she exuded such class that you couldn't tell when we were struggling. From her table settings to the meticulous way she kept everything *just* in place, you would have thought we lived on Park Avenue instead of in Park Heights. She was the only person I knew that could make liver look so good that she could convince you it was as good as steak.

My mother demanded excellence in how we talked, walked, and looked. That was how she inspired us. Education was championed in my home as much as hard work was. My parents believed that whatever you do, it must be done with everything you have. I'm not sure what their professional desires were for me, but I know they wanted me to thrive, no matter what path I chose. They didn't want any of their kids to be stuck in survival mode. They instilled in us the truth that possessions are transitory; who we are and the good we leave behind us are eternal.

It seemed like my father was always on the road. But the

moments that I did get to spend with him still linger with me today. Climbing in his truck was an adventure all on its own. I would tag along with him on his runs for a day or two. The best trips were by surprise. Sometimes he would look at me in the morning and say, "Do you want to go to school or with me?"

Was there a question? No way! These were typically one-day runs to Philadelphia or New York. *Breaker breaker 1-2* is the phrase we would send off on the radio, letting other CB users know we were rolling and available for communication. My dad's handle was the Godfather, and mine was the Little Don. Once we got our load, I would pull the horn, my greatest thrill.

It's amazing what a young man can learn by doing. Every mile marker we passed looked like an emerald in our mirrors—a sign letting me know that I got to choose who I could be and where I would go.

One night riding back home, we saw a rig swaying back and forth on the road. I asked my dad if that guy was drunk. His reply continues to be a mainstay for me: "He's not drunk; he's a dream weaver." (A dream weaver is a truck driver trying to make up time and falling asleep at the wheel.) "Your life is more important than the load you carry, Michael."

For some reason that wisdom went straight to my heart. Your dreams cannot show up unless you do, and sometimes we carry a load that feels so chaotic, so urgent, that it puts us and others at risk.

We honked our horn, trying to let the drifter know he was in danger. Thankfully he pulled over, and we passed him into the night.

As I became older, those trips occurred less often. My dad's own dreams had begun to materialize. He was ahead of his time—going from driving a truck to running a megachurch in the '80s, hosting his own radio show (called *The Pastor's Corner*), and overseeing a burgeoning education and missions organization.

As my great-aunt Edna would eventually say to me, "Preaching is in your DNA." Four generations of preachers are in my family: my great-grandfather, my grandparents, my parents, and me. Most of my grandmother's siblings were in ministry in some way. We would often joke about the familial irony: you were either a preacher or a problem. Our family was like any family showing the dichotomy that some people are on right paths and some are on the wrong path. In love with Jesus or in a relationship with gin and juice.

My grandmother was the matriarch of the family: Cécilia Thomas, fair-skinned like Dorothy Dandridge but as tough as Harriett Tubman. She was a private nurse and a praying woman. I never knew my father's father.

My grandmother remarried a Baptist preacher, Bishop Reginald Thomas, a dark-skinned, well-dressed man. She was

African Methodist Episcopal, but after they got married, they started the Rock of Ages Pentecostal Church—one of those washboard, tambourine, and Hammond-B3-organ-blaring-in-the-background types. It started out in a storefront on Sharp Street, but eventually they built a new edifice on Rogers Avenue from the ground up. It's still there today.

My father became the pastor of Rock of Ages in 1979 and knew that the status quo would never accommodate his dreams for the congregation. He had a vision to start a Christian school with classes from kindergarten to the twelfth grade. He wanted to create a hub of hope where a church and a school could both serve the community and stand as a model to solve the systemic issues of the "village" of our neighborhood.

I will never forget the day he saw the building where he would eventually put this school and church. We were driving down Hilton Street in his big brown Cadillac: leather seats, sunroof top, gangster whitewall tires. Suddenly he turned his head and stopped the car in the middle of the street. He got out. I followed my father, standing in the road.

He stood staring at an immense abandoned building in front of us, all while cars squeezed by, people honking and calling us all sorts of names.

My father ignored it all. He studied the building, mesmerized. He stood in silence for five minutes, then climbed back into the Cadillac.

"Dad, what's wrong?" I asked as I closed the door and he shifted into gear.

The look on my dad's face didn't signal any type of concern. Instead, he seemed excited. Dreaming.

A couple of weeks later, my father got a tour of the building that had entranced him, and I joined him. As it turns out, at one time this had been the most expensive school that had ever been built in Baltimore. The 158,000-square-foot building was constructed in the 1920s in what was then a middle-class district neighborhood. When it became integrated in the late '50s, like what was happening in most urban communities, the White people left. There were not enough students to populate the massive space, so the city closed the school. By the time we were going through it, it had long stood empty. We walked through the echoing, empty space, and it was as if I could see my father fill each room with his eyes. He could see some potential invisible to others in the rundown building.

"We're going to move the church here," he said. "This is where we start the school."

And that's exactly what he did. My father was able to lease it from the mayor.

A year later we moved into the building.

"Okay, go clean the bathroom." These were *not* the words I expected to hear when I told my father I had decided to follow in his footsteps as a pastor. But I'm getting ahead of my-self. . . .

Right after my father acquired the building that he wanted to have for his church, everybody worked hard to get it ready for the opening Sunday service.

One day we were there while workers were putting down carpet. There was a lot of commotion, with people going back and forth amid the giant rolls of carpet on the floor. I was standing behind the stage, looking out at my father who was speaking to someone, and I suddenly felt the urge to tell him my newfound aspiration. I walked over to him and tugged at his shirt, but he kept talking. Soon my pestering made him look down, wondering what was wrong.

"I want to be a preacher," I said.

My father stopped everything he was doing and began looking around.

"Give me a moment," he said to me.

My father walked to the corner of the room, came back holding a mop, and then handed it to me.

"Okay, go clean the bathroom," my father told me.

I nodded. I didn't think much about it as I went to the bathroom to start cleaning. I cleaned that bathroom like my name was Mr. Clean. I not only mopped the floor, but I also scrubbed the toilet bowls and scoured the sinks and wiped down the mirrors. When my father came back a few hours later, he gave me a nod of approval.

"You're going to be a *great* preacher someday," he said.

"Why?" I didn't understand.

"Because if you're willing to clean a bathroom, you can preach to people."

This was my father's way of simplifying a truth. He was telling me that if you're going to preach the gospel, then you're going to have to get used to being in the mess. You're going to have to get used to taking the humble role of being able to share the good news with people without telling them how to run their lives and without giving a judgmental glance at what their lives look like. "Clean the bathroom" clarified this in a way that stuck with me forever.

"The turntables might wobble, but they don't fall down." It was the summer of 1986. Every radio was blasting Run-DMC's "Peter Piper." The iconic "Hell's Bells" in the song were blaring in the background as we left for an impromptu family trip. My dad took the whole family on the road from Maryland to California and back. For four amazing weeks, we traveled to twenty-seven states and saw almost everything we could. There was something prophetic about the way my father wanted us to have this experience.

He modeled a global perspective of thought. He often talked about and researched other countries. He made me intrigued about what life was like on the continent of Africa and the divergent cultures of its fifty-four countries. But his intensity for our sudden departure around the country was striking. It was as if he knew he was running out of time.

There is more available than what you have experienced.

We were suddenly exposed to so much.

The soaring stainless steel of the Gateway Arch in St. Louis, lifting 630 feet to the sky.

The staring faces of our national history carved in granite rock at Mount Rushmore National Memorial in the Black Hills of South Dakota.

The broken crack of the Liberty Bell in Philadelphia, where we ate the best cheesesteaks you'll ever have.

The breathtaking wilderness and wildlife of Yellowstone National Park in Wyoming, Montana, and Idaho.

The towering trio of steeples at the St. Louis Cathedral in New Orleans.

We drove across the Golden Gate Bridge and visited Alcatraz Island in the San Francisco area before traveling to see the immense trees in the redwood forests. We stared out onto one of the Great Lakes and saluted the Statue of Liberty.

It was an unforgettable experience, as my father knew it would be. Taking a helicopter ride over the Grand Canyon, a kid from Park Heights was suddenly flying high over God's artistry. This was the stuff of fantasy and fables, pulling us out of the world we were in and exposing us to environments we never thought we would experience.

Having sight without a vision is a dangerous way to walk through life. A false view of what you have seen can cause you to miss the opportunities ahead, making it impossible to imagine a world beyond your own. The trip was Dad's gift to us. It was almost as if he knew what was coming, as if he knew he needed to show us as much as possible before we would suffer another blow.

Hiding behind my father's wisdom were his own wounds. He was sick but hadn't told us. His severe case of hypertension was one thing, but after injuring his leg playing basketball, he developed a blood clot. He walked around with a limp for nine months as the blood clot traveled from his leg to his brain. Immediately after our trip, my father was admitted to Mercy Hospital. He suffered a stroke and heart attack and slipped into a coma.

Weeks passed. My mother was staying at a hotel called the Tremont Plaza right across the street. When the car I was riding in pulled up to the hotel, I climbed out and walked into the crowded lobby. I immediately began to recognize individuals from our church.

They all had looks of bereavement on their faces.

I knew something bad had happened, but I didn't linger to ask someone. The elevator felt like it took an eternity to reach the suite my mother was in. When I stepped in the room, I could see my grandmother sitting down and other family members standing around talking. Someone told me my mother was in the bedroom, so I walked in to see her. She immediately ushered me into the bathroom, closed the door, and told me.

My father was dead.

I no longer had my greatest model. The ground beneath me swallowed me whole. Darkness was all I felt as the remaining light of hope succumbed to the collapse of my heart. *What happens now?* In that suspended moment, I knew I would not be well, not for some time.

CHAPTER FOUR

Bitter Seed

Everything I ever learned that mattered, I learned it
from failure and falling and suffering. I celebrated
success, but I learned it in suffering.

—Bishop T. D. Jakes

The hurricane in my soul was roaring as I sat in a pew of
my father's church and heard the words of the speaker
addressing a crowd dressed in black: "The Lord gives, and
the Lord takes away. . . ."

I was twelve years old. I heard the preacher shout these
words without any understanding of the context. All I could
hear, all I could feel, was that the Lord had taken away. Did
anything else matter?

I suppose I was searching for someone to blame. That was
the only way I could make any sense out of the feeling of

being utterly betrayed. The preacher served as the prosecutor. I was judge and jury. God was the defendant, and I could not wait for the verdict to come.

Like dark wood adorning a courtroom, my father's funeral was tragically beautiful. You couldn't get a seat in the church, packed full of those mourning the loss of a great man. It was a celebration and testament to Richard Phillips. But I wondered if anyone could see the pain hidden under my mother's best church hat.

The church sang so forcefully that it felt like Jesus was coming down to join us in the celebration of my father's life. Several preachers spoke, but the only one I really paid attention to was the reverend who quoted Job's words: "The Lord gives, and the Lord takes away."

I don't know if the Lord gives, but I sure know the Lord takes away, I thought.

In context, Job said those words to process and describe his response to the pain he was going through; *God* didn't say them. Yet that was the way I understood those words as the preacher explained them—that was how they became etched in my mind and my heart.

The official diagnosis on my father was that a blood clot from his leg traveled to his brain and burst, causing a stroke that in turn caused a heart attack. But at that moment I was convinced that the true cause and culprit behind his death was God. *He* took my father. The Lord took away.

A seed was sown. As soon as it fell, bitterness germinated,

spreading in me. Seeds do not ask for permission. I could not disregard the preacher. My heart was overwhelmed by the absence of God's help and the hubris of the reverend's words.

"The Lord gives, and the Lord takes away."

Oh, really? Is that right? Well, I don't think I want to serve a God who does that.

The power shut off. Just like that, the bright promise of wanting to follow in my father's footsteps suddenly turned black. I didn't want to have anything to do with God. When the inner storm was over, all that was left was agony and agnosticism.

Grief is not a single emotion. Nor is it a single event. Grief is a cycle. When we have loss enter our lives, we can feel displaced. Dislocated, disenfranchised, discombobulated, and everything in between. Our faith can feel disorganized, and it can be hard to get our bearings. A storm is raging, and it's hard for us to see where we are. When we have those experiences, we often fail to rest on the guiding and eternal barometers of our souls to show the way out. Instead, we can look to things for guidance that have no steady course of their own—or that even may be leading us further out from a safe harbor.

In such times, it's difficult not to allow rage to impact the order of our souls. The storm on the inside often feels far more powerful than the storm on the outside. And we all end up dealing with such storms in our own ways.

I thought the storm inside me would end when I struck

the gavel in my mind and declared God guilty. But of course it didn't.

Most nights, I could hear my mother crying. I sat outside her closed bedroom door, feeling powerless. I could find no words or hope to offer her. She never showed those tears to her children but instead shed them when she was by herself. Listening to her weep not only made me feel helpless, but it also somehow intensified the betrayal curling deep inside me.

My hero was gone.

Everything I aspired to be, everything I looked up to . . . *gone.*

And to make things worse, my father wasn't the only one who was gone. My brother had taken off after the burial.

He had just walked off. Literally. He didn't get into the limo. It would be some time before I saw him again. His absence was a constant reminder of the loss that had devastated our home.

My sisters dealt with the sorrow in their ways too. Though it looked different for each of us, we all ended up making bad choices. My father's death sent a lightning bolt through our family, ripping us apart, but that's the nature of trauma. It interrupts the plotline.

I played it all over and over again in my mind. I couldn't understand how Dad could die. He was a preacher. He was

God's man. He cared for people. He did all these wonderful things. It just didn't make any *sense*. Why him? Why then? No answers.

I was crushed, confused, and alone. I had nobody to ask questions of or to talk to about my father's death. There was no therapy back then—at least not in the Black community—and in those days, counseling was still a taboo subject in the church. Of course, now we could have had family therapy or grief counseling, but back then we didn't have any of that. You didn't go to therapy; you went to church.

Everybody in the community said what they were going to do. How they would reach out to our family, come around us in support. How they were going to be there for us. I never expected it would really materialize, and it didn't. People mean well and try to do their best. But, you know, any of us can get caught up in our natural arcs of life, because we are all dealing with something.

I never met my grandfather. I had often wondered how my dad felt about the void that had been left by his own missing father, but he never talked about it. During the funeral, a man had come up to the casket to see my dad, and my godmother had whispered in my ear, "That man's your grandfather." I looked at the stranger as he walked by us, slowly shuffling his feet, head hung down, holding his old-man hat. He never looked up, never said a word to anybody. He left—didn't even stay for the whole thing. I didn't ever have to wonder what shame looked like because that day it walked past me slow enough for a good, long look.

And in the middle of it all, my mother did what Black women have been doing for eternity. She held everything together. A thirty-five-year-old widow and mom with four kids did the impossible: she kept our family going. There was no time for her to tell us about the grown folks' business—that my father hadn't taken care of his health, that he had no life insurance or retirement savings. She didn't tell us that the bills were coming due. She was always the backbone of our family, but now she had to be the leader of my father's church, too, holding everyone together. Watching that drama unfold made it all the more difficult for me to reinvest my heart in what used to be meaningful.

The one resource I had, what my family would come to depend on the most, was my mother's prayers and her persistence to press on. She used to say, "I'm not going to let the Enemy have my seed," but I believed she feared that the tares had already been added to the wheat. All she could do, like the old parable, was let the crop and weeds grow up together. While she waited, she would fight. Prayer is not a fair weapon. My mother was a prayer warrior, and those prayers got us through these times. I wish I had realized the power of her spiritual weapons; I would need them much later in my life.

My mother's anxiety and pain were real. But so was her hope. So was her faith. She didn't deny the reality that had come down, but she did redefine it.

In contrast, I was convinced that what I thought deep in my heart was true: *none of us are going to make it.*

Not without Dad.

Learning was the last thing on my mind after my father died. I returned to school wounded, furious, and defiant. I wanted to try to move forward. I wanted to try to be the student I knew I could be, but with no positive relationships with adults in my school, that was difficult. There was no space in my student profile that suggested that my father had passed. There was no line in my profile that described my trauma history.

My first day at school, after a wild summer, was an epic disaster. I came that day holding my notebook, but I left in handcuffs. It was the first time I had ever been "arrested." I thought about the irony of being locked up at school after all the things I did on the streets, because to me school felt like a prison anyway. I was detained for the serious offense of being defiant. The vaguely defined charge was enough to have three police officers come to our building, all because another kid and I exchanged a few words and when the assistant principal told us to clear the hall, we didn't. It was a nonviolent exchange that was described as a gang conflict.

My innocence was gone and replaced with an active and simmering ambivalence. What was I going to do with my pain? The way I processed it was by doing dumb stuff out on the streets. I started hanging out on the corners a little bit more, delivering packages here and there for people. I knew they held drugs, but I didn't care. I stole my first car that year. Some old guy left his keys in the ignition, so I hopped in and took it. One thing led to another, in slow steps that seemed to move only in one direction—the wrong one. There was no amount of willpower that I could muster to stop doing dumb stuff. The more stuff I did, the greater the rewards: a little money in my pocket and a lot of clout along the way.

Before long, it was seeming to pay off. *Look at my bedroom wall lined with sneakers.* Every color of Nike Air Force 1s and, close to the end, a batch of Baltimore's most iconic kicks: fresh white Reebok Classics.

Weeks passed, then months. The streets became my sanctuary. The drug dealers on the corners became my pastors. They led me faithfully every week to darker pastures. We shared the same sense of abandonment. We were the disinherited, a band of brothers that didn't break for nobody.

The life had appeal for a smart, industrious kid. There was more innovation out there than I would ever experience in a classroom. There was more opportunity out there than school had to offer. I came to love the streets, and in their hard way, the streets loved me back. There wasn't any real glory in what we were doing, but the sense of belonging was enough to make us believe there was.

If I had done the math, the low probability of making it

out of my lifestyle alive would have changed my mind, but sadly I was ready to die. If you got pinched, it was a badge of honor. If you got shot, it was a stripe added to your shoulder. If Five-O caught you with a heater and you did a mandatory five-year bit, you were celebrated on the other side. The only thing that kept me from completely giving in to the deadly fallacy of bullets and jumpsuits was the positive people who remained around me. Although I often felt alone, I wasn't.

So as I grew into a young man, I decided to live in two worlds: the world of faith my father had just left and the secular one that was always waiting for me. The street became my space to empty out my pain. The church became the perfect place to camouflage what I did on the street.

But living that way was stressful. When people would say in church that "trouble doesn't always last" or "God is a healer," those words carried an emotional connotation that reminded me of my loss. When someone would say on the street that he didn't believe he'd live to see twenty-one, my response was silence. Those words created an emotional conflict, because though I'd bought the lie that I was ready to meet my maker, I truly wanted to *live*. What I wish I understood back then was the cumulative wounding that occurs in our words, because we are often speaking to people who are dealing with more than we realize.

Maya Angelou said this about words: "Words are things, I'm convinced. You must be careful about the words you use or the words you allow to be used in your house." The words I heard in the church had a profound effect on me and not in a good way.

I was a kid dealing with a whole list of traumatic issues and no language for it—just labels and judgment. "He's gone bad." "Why aren't you more like your father?" "Church boy."

When trauma goes unacknowledged, tragedy goes uninterrupted.

Being able to articulate what's going on with you is very important, because if you don't, you're going to store it. And when you store your pain, you can't transform it. Pain is not something that you are supposed to go through; it's supposed to go through you. If you can learn how to let it pass, then you can get the payoff for it. Otherwise you become a carrier affecting others with your hurt.

Stored pain is intractable and pervasive, but it is noticeable by its effects. I began to notice it in people all around me. There may be no visible wheelchairs or crutches that indicate it, just words and behavior that serve as giveaways. I saw it in the hunched-over lady on the bus stop, nodding with that junkie lean. I saw it in the police officers' eyes as they rolled up on the block to harass whomever they could find. I saw it in the hustlers sporting it around their necks and wrists disguised as bling. I saw it in the blue-collar men going into the liquor store to get a pack of smokes and a bottle. I saw it in the single moms at the grocery store using their food stamps to purchase food for their babies, hoping that no one they knew would notice they were on government assistance. I saw it in myself.

But I never saw it in my mom.

She made us go to church every Sunday—a commitment. Our service was like four hours long. I showed up numb and hollow, but I did enjoy playing the drums. I could see everyone from the platform.

Like on the streets, I saw hurting people. But how they handled their hurt was different. They lifted their hands. They shouted, not vocally but rather stepping rapidly, one foot down after the other to the unforced rhythm of grace. They clapped their hands in unison, sounding like one big snare drum. They cried. They even ran around the church as if they were letting something out—or letting something in. Then I realized it: *this is what they do with their pain.* I understood that not one of us is meant to bear our burdens alone. To try to do so is an awful presumption. I wanted to join them so badly. But I couldn't. In hindsight, my refusal to feel God's presence would let me be only a bystander. From time to time, tears would form in some of those "the Lord is here" services, but I was unwilling to intervene in my own turmoil. I shook it off.

As C. S. Lewis said, "A man can no more diminish God's glory by refusing to worship Him than a lunatic can put out the sun by scribbling the word 'darkness' on the walls of his cell."

Just like that, I realized that I wanted to experience real

freedom. I also recognized that I didn't want to be a criminal. I was more like Gordon Gekko than like John Gotti. I wasn't tough; I was calculating. I was *scared,* and where I was, that was more dangerous than anything else.

Fear and pain have an inextricable link. When we try our best to avoid suffering, we end up suffering for it. The immutable irony of anguish is that we cannot carry it; suffering carries us, inevitably leading us to the one place we don't want to go: back to God. Whom else can we question when we go through difficult times? I questioned, "Why me?" I said "We don't deserve this," but what I really wanted to know was "What kind of God are You?" I skipped the blaming others bit and went straight to the source but would not discover an answer for some time. I easily mistook God's silence for His absence, and I let the pain pull me down into the darkness. When you're falling, you don't think about the bottom. You don't imagine what awaits you. You just want to catch your breath. There is no time to rebuke the suffering; I couldn't if I tried. You just have to keep breathing. What was counterintuitive about it all was that the suffering, the pain, forced me to let go of my grip on a small self-serving explanation. Being forced to go to church gave me enough light that I began to trust the darkness.

Faith is patience with mystery.

I don't know how it happened, but I began to embrace the uncertainty of it all. I stopped asking questions. I just wanted to live. What I discovered falling down is that there is a foundation at the bottom. Once there, instead of pulling me out of shattered expectations, God would meet me in the rubble. The bottom is where I learned some of my greatest lessons on how to distill wisdom from the waste places.

Trials are master teachers. They instruct you on how to build new understandings.

I had to tear down all the negativity that I had constructed in my mind. Grieving is a renovation project. Smashing the walls and pulling out the fixtures are fun until you see the mess and have to live inside the debris. Facing the brokenness painfully strips away the comfort of concealment, but it ultimately leads to healing. In my mind I started to argue with the facts that were in opposition of hope, because fear provides just as much evidence as faith does. My soul was laid bare like an unfinished basement, but my resolve was stacked up like drywall waiting to be placed on the frame of my purpose. I used the raw material that hope provided to fashion a makeshift mental fence signaling to my environment and my grief in all its cruelty, "No trespassing." Grief always precedes growth. Whether it's a muscle, a mindset, or a habit, something is going to be sacrificed for new development to take place.

Whatever we do habitually will always have the power to defeat what happens occasionally. The street—my hood—was not in my DNA, but it was in my zip code. The persona of being a tough guy was a habit that I formed. I wasn't really built like that, but I became convinced that I had to be like that to survive. I had to learn to let that persona go. I had some resources that I could depend on, I had a family, and I had had a father. Though he had died, he'd shown me enough to know that there was a different way. He'd shown me a world far beyond our neighborhood. There were kids that I grew up with who had fewer options than I did, who had less support than I did, who were really out on those street corners trying to take care of a little sister or an addicted parent. There were kids who had worse plights but rejected annihilation, affirming their right to live. They got up every day and went to school in hopes of a better future. I made a bad choice about who I would be.

I'm thankful today that it didn't kill me.

"It is easier to build strong children than to repair broken men." Back then, my school experience did not accept that statement widely attributed to Frederick Douglass. I was suspended for five days over heated words; the other kid got two weeks. The school was more interested in our guilt than our growth. They had a zero-tolerance policy that was all stick and no carrot. Policies like this ensure that communities will spend a lot of time and money repairing adults. Over time as I progressed through school, cops didn't show up when there was a conflict; they were already there.

How did we go from the image of a student putting an apple on the teacher's desk to the decision of lawmakers to put armed police officers into our schools? Have our apples fallen that far from the tree, or could it be that we planted the wrong policies? Our misconceptions around school discipline and safety grow from the kernel of insufficient knowledge and the stem of misguided wisdom.

The public perceived the increased involvement of school-based law enforcement officers as an improvement in youth crime, particularly school shootings, in the early 1990s. Many feared that street crime was spilling over to our schools from our communities. Schools with disruptive conduct trends were clustered in neighborhoods characterized as disadvantaged and economically disorganized. The federal government started to enact laws like the 1994 Gun-Free Schools Act in reaction to the public's concern that teens might become increasingly violent. This federal act ended the discretionary aspect of school rules and implemented formal disciplinary standards, such as zero-tolerance policies—a practice that became ubiquitous across the country. The attempt to clamp down on the "violence" in schools became an extension of our criminal justice system.

Looking back now, I see that Black and Brown people are not inherently violent, but many of their circumstances are. Adverse community environments cannot be uncoupled from adverse childhood experiences. While the family is a child's first influence, there is no way to separate those families from the communities in which they live. Violence in and of itself is not the problem; voicelessness is. Beneath it all are hurt communities that certain policies have not helped. Hurt cannot be healed until it is heard. When no one is making laws from the communities' perspective, it becomes easy to champion consequential policies rather than promote restorative practices.

When we suspend young kids, even kindergarteners, we've made it clear that criminalization and overdisciplining are a higher priority than learning and support. Still, too many schools are focused on administering harsh corrective outcomes rather than engaging in "preventive and holistic strategies that will foster positive learning climates, reduce student misbehavior, and promote academic achievement." The school-to-prison pipeline (the invisible structures that move young people, disproportionately young men of color, straight from school into prison) exists because of these types of laws. Without the necessary shade that adults should be providing, our children will never truly be safe or supported. If we choose to facilitate this "combination of factors: overly harsh 'zero tolerance' discipline policies and practices; consequential and biased disciplinary decisions by teachers and administrators; increased police presence in schools, criminalization of trivial code of conduct violations; and segregated and under resourced schools," then we will always build more prisons than schools. We will always have to repair more adults.

We should use innovative learning approaches to discipline "that build strong relationships, foster inclusive and positive learning environments, and hold students accountable for misconduct in rehabilitative ways that improve future behavior." Instruction, not punishing, is the aim of discipline. "The Latin roots for discipline include *discipulus* which means pupil or student and *disciplina* which means teaching or learning."

We need an army of counselors, not cops. With the obvious advantages of engaging in student mental health services, it would make sense for school boards, local legislators, and federal officials to use all available resources to improve school-based health providers. But that's not the trend. Instead, there has been an increase in police funding in schools, while our schools face a critical shortage of counselors, nurses, psychologists, and social workers. Approximately eight million students are without at least one of these supports, but they all have police in their schools. That's 20 percent of our student population who do not have the proper support. Conversely, there is zero evidence that an increase in police presence in schools produces positive outcomes.

I'm not arguing that police don't have a place in our society; they certainly do, but schools are not the ideal location apart from other supports. We should consider planting restorative approaches on purpose by placing community liaisons picked from the very neighborhoods that we've identified as problematic. We can train those individuals and implement a continuum of restorative approaches and strategies such as community conferencing, conflict management, restorative circles, mindfulness exercises, and social-emotional curricula.

If we truly value our children, it will be reflected in our decision-making and our practices, ensuring equitable outcomes for all.

I never wanted to leave the city. I loved where I was from. With all of its challenges, it was home. But my mother could read the tea leaves. She didn't want to have to come and identify her child's body at the morgue. So just shy of a year after my father's death, she moved us to Columbia, Maryland—which felt a world away from Park Heights.

I hated it. I'd never seen that many White people in my life. We were the only Black family in our cul-de-sac. It was a different kind of adversity than what I'd known in Baltimore. While I had experienced adversity based on the color of my skin, this kind of racial trauma felt new to me. The day we moved in, you would have thought we were aliens from outer space who had pulled up in a UFO instead of a U-Haul. This wasn't the same as the glaring discrimination that my grandmother endured or that my uncles talked about, but it was still painful. It manifested as hurtful skepticism. Like we didn't belong.

My mother had a big smile on her face as she took the time to speak to every neighbor. I stood next to her, going from house to house, and wondered why she was being so nice. At the end, it was as if she could read what I was thinking. "We've come too far to allow a few looks to stop us, Michael," she said. "Pick your head up, and go in the house."

On the surface, Columbia looked like a cultural utopia. All the parks and pathways were connected, and the town was broken up into villages that remained tethered through the Columbia Association. You got an ID card, and with that in hand, you could go to any fitness club, bowling alley, or skating rink. Even the one movie theater that was there at the time allowed you to get discounts with the association card. It was culture shock, to put it mildly. I was cut off from the things that I was familiar with. There was no corner store. No police car sirens. No one spoke the way I did. The suburbs felt like living in a foreign country.

My sisters loved it, but I was the only male in the house. All I wanted to do was to go to my grandmother's since she still lived in the city. *This is crazy,* I thought. *I cannot live out here.*

My mother gave me the room in the basement to cheer me up. It was like having my own apartment. I could see the community pool right across the street from our back patio. On the very first day after moving in, I threw on my trunks, grabbed a towel, and walked over with my brand-new Columbia Association ID. Kids were playing a game of fifty with this basketball hoop in the pool. It was the first time I'd ever seen such a thing. I was eager to join the game. I quickly scored fifty points, with each basket counting as five; then I selected the first person I wanted to put out of the game. After making the basket, the kid called me out by my name followed by the N-word. This kid shoved me and splashed water in my face, so I drilled him. Suddenly there was this big up-roar.

"The Black kid just punched him in the face!"

The lifeguard came around and got me out of the pool, telling me I had to leave and couldn't come back.

"What do you mean I have to leave?" I asked. "He hit me first."

It sucks to be the "only." Walking back across the street with me were the feelings of total embarrassment and confusion. I punched him, but he got the better of me. I felt like being a Black kid in Columbia was like swimming with weights. They might as well have pushed me to the bottom of the pool and held me there. When I got home, I was angry and full of tears and told my mom how I wanted to leave.

Society can be a bully. It can be violent against *you*, but you get punished if you even *think* about retaliating.

My mother calmed me down by explaining the power of being the only Black family or the only Black kid at the pool. "You get to tear down the concepts that people hold as true," she told me. "You get to show them how valuable you are. Being the only is not a weakness—it's a strength."

By the next day, I was at the pool again and everything was fine. When I got there, one of the adults walked up to me and said he had seen me playing yesterday. I was dreading what would come next. But then, "You're a phenomenal athlete," he said. I let out a breath that I didn't know I had been holding. "Have you considered playing on any of the local teams?" he continued.

It was painfully obvious to me that I needed to find a place to put my pain.

And as it turns out, sports would be the perfect place.

CHAPTER FIVE

Walking Without Purpose

You see us as you want to see us—in the simplest
terms, in the most convenient definitions.
—Anthony Michael Hall, as Brian Johnson
in *The Breakfast Club*

The narrative arc of my life changed when my identity
shifted from troubled youth to talented athlete. Instead
of walking the path of least resistance, I was running down
the road to becoming a competitor. I had something to go for.
My innate drive for achievement needed a place to thrive because the streets were not going to offer me a positive outcome. I became immersed in sports, and suddenly my worth
at school increased, but to me it was indistinguishable from
the value that I had on the street. My school was affluent and
predominantly White. I found the unexpected embrace to be

inauthentic. The precipitous love that I had received from guys around my neighborhood when I did something wrong, like boosting a car or selling weed, mirrored the newfound pats on the back that my school was giving me. Both communities required conformity for me to be welcomed.

Prior to my athletic discovery, I was perceived as a threat, inside and outside school. As a young Black male, I was made to feel unwelcome regardless of where I showed up, a misfit who was expendable because of the belief that I was not a core member of the community and the assumption that I would not be a positive contributor to society. Many times I would be harassed by an officer or have the police called on me for walking down the street or for riding my bike through a different neighborhood. I would find myself in the office at school or suspended for the same behavior as my non-Black peers, but the consequences for me were different.

I was raised to speak up for myself, to respectfully question authority, and to be a critical thinker. These characteristics are normally valued in our society, yet I was often criticized and a few times almost criminalized for displaying them. It was extremely difficult for me to navigate the gaps between the culture in my home and the culture in my school. I was not prepared for the social diversity that I was being exposed to, and I certainly was not being educated on it. But now there I was, in a predominately White suburban school, being celebrated because of my raw athletic talent.

Performing athletically was like having a tacit agreement

between the school and myself. If I gave them my physical talents to entertain them, then no objection would be made to my potential. But if I told the powers that be what was on my mind, if I shared my ideas or rather the pain that was in my heart, then the circumstances of our undisclosed, nonnegotiable contract would change. I felt as if I was silently being told to shut up and dribble and that for me to make it up the social ladder, I would have to submit to the imbalance of power that seems to be an intractable force in our society.

We are all more complex than our classifications. We are more layered than the labels placed on us. People are put into boxes to help others understand them, but every individual is more multifaceted than that. A label is something you slap on top of a surface or product; unfortunately we have a culture that prefers to stick all kinds of unfair and misrepresented labels onto our souls. In this case, being labeled as just an athlete would be one more moniker I had to live with.

From early childhood, I had to fight back. I had to peel off the demeaning epithets forced on me by society while simultaneously dealing with the silent inferences of inferiority that came as a standard feature in our culture. But by the time I got to high school, my aggravation with that consistent conflict, coupled with trying to survive in my fragile ecosystem, was making me hostile toward everyone. Playing sports gave shelter to the aggression that society was creating in me. Getting after it with tenacity and viciousness was admired and rewarded. It's amazing how people can praise you without knowing that your performance is predicated by your pain. Running fast and jumping high opened the door for me to rapidly be deemed as a nonthreat and incidentally became my way out of hurt and harm's way. Even the guys around my neighborhood began to protect me because I was a baller. Everything I went through was the fuel I used to become tenacious on the field and on the court.

Athletics is an honest space. As you move up, there is a natural progression of finding out very quickly where you stand. Either you can do this or learn how, or you're not built for it. The goal of athletic candor is not to dash dreams but to set achievable expectations. You're not going to spend a lot of time trying to do something that you can't. But if you have the seeds of greatness for a sport and you're willing to work your butt off, you'll get a lot of help. It's hard to look anyone in the eye and say, "You're average." With sports you don't have to. It provides instant feedback but still offers glimmers of hope, and no hope is ever too small.

Pop Warner football gave me the first glimpse of how far I could go athletically. I played football for a team called the Columbia Cobras. They had equipment for every player—helmets, shoulder pads, and all the accessories—and that was just at tryouts. In the bustle on the field, it seemed like they had more position coaches than an NFL team. I was used to one or maybe two coaches in the city leagues; oh, and you'd be lucky if you had kneepads.

Lack has a funny way of making you become loyal to very

little, misinforming you to think that not having what you need is the way things will always be. Putting on my new equipment was therapeutic. When I buckled my chinstrap and snapped it into place, it felt like my world had gotten bigger. I felt like I had significance. I began to hope again. I began to dream again. I made the team that year as a running back. Maybe things were going to be okay.

My coach identified me as a leader, as somebody with heart, grit, and raw talent. So he, along with my teammates, made me a team captain. It meant more than they could know. This was my first taste at becoming a leader in a positive setting, and I loved it. Self-esteem can be built, and sports gave me the skill set to slowly rebuild mine.

While football was my first love, I excelled at basketball. I remember making my first hoop out of a milk crate in Park Heights, using a piece of wood for the backboard and climbing the telephone pole to hang it so we could play a game of horse. It was the real hardwood, though, that provided me the fortitude to embrace my own potential. I found meaning on the court, and meaning began to reveal purpose.

I got to hoop with elite players, which was a revelation to me. I belonged. I was good enough to compete with some of the best. It gave me a deep sense of achievement and planted the idea that this was going to be my ticket—my passport to the world. When you have hoop dreams, contingencies never enter your mind.

I thought I was going to make it.

The determination to become a pro athlete was a ubiquitous idea in my environment. Thinking about going to college was not the cultural norm—certainly not for me, and I don't believe it was for most of my friends either, unless they were athletes. For many of us, that was the perception: that the few shots we had toward upward mobility were through either sports or crime. Realizing just how potent I was at basketball, I began to think about how I could get a scholarship. Perhaps if I ran hard enough or jumped high enough, I could cross over the gaps of inequity. With faith, even if it was the size of a mustard seed, I went after it.

For my achievements on the basketball court, I was invited to the esteemed Five-Star Basketball Camp. Howard Garfinkel himself, the legend that started the camp, told me I was going to be playing at the next level. I made the all-star team that year and was invited back each year as a future college prospect.

Things were good. I had a forty-inch vertical, averaged over twenty points a game, and ran a sub-4.5 seconds in the forty-yard dash and 22.9 seconds in the two-hundred-yard sprint. But it wasn't until my senior year that someone would note my *intellectual* potential or talk with me about the prospects of going to college on its own merits. The athletic director of my school called me into his office to tell me how intelligent he thought I was and that I should seriously consider going to college and applying for an academic scholarship. I thought he was joking. I'd never heard that from an adult in school before. For years I had been told I would end up in jail or amount to nothing. He continued, telling me that he'd sent out videotapes of me to dozens of Division I schools but wanted me to know that *beyond* my athletic ability I had plenty more to show. With that said, he dumped all the recruitment letters on the desk.

I stared. *My passport to the world is in that pile.*

Mr. Harris, smiling on the other side of his desk, was the coolest White man I had ever met. He had a chiseled face like a young Mel Gibson but the old-man swag of Sean Connery. He often stopped me in the hall to talk and cheered for me at games. I really didn't know how to respond to the kind words he often expressed, but I knew they were real.

While I was still standing in his office, he asked one of the school counselors to come in. Immediately she began to encourage me about going to college. Mrs. Robinson was an older Black lady with regal gray hair and silky skin. The only wrinkles she had were around her eyes that told the story that she had seen it all. She reminded me of my academic accomplishments and intellectual attributes. She told me that I had a 3.9 GPA and that I had a strong enough score on my SAT (even though I hadn't studied for it and had been out all night partying before taking the test early in the morning because I just didn't think that it mattered).

Mrs. Robinson held my hand and told me over and over again, "Michael, you're smart. Michael, you're smart." I so wanted to believe her. But it was high school—and to my memory, the first time in my life that an adult had told me I was smart. It was odd to hear her talking. The idea of being academically viable was antithetical to the experiences I had up until that point. That I might have worth based on something other than athletics wasn't something I'd considered. Strangely, it bothered me to think about it. Mrs. Robinson's kind words landed on me like pesky insects. I tried to shake them off. I didn't value that aspect of me, nor did I have the skill to be critically conscious enough to know how much the forces of privilege, oppression, and trauma had caused me to deny my own agency as a person. Of course I was more than an athlete. But I couldn't accept that fact.

I've never had an idea I didn't love. For dreamers like myself, dreaming big is a feature that comes naturally. For those of us who've never thought small but were only made to feel small by the people and the systems that were charged with bringing out our innate possibilities, there is a sense of betrayal that sticks to our souls. The level of those disappointments can make us forget who we are.

We are told to go to school because education is the pathway toward social mobility and a tool for liberation. In school, we spend significant time being shaped by people who may or may not believe that we are capable of our true potential. The people I encountered in my schooling who did not believe I had intellectual potential were not malicious. But they were ignorant. They weren't out to harm me, but their lack of cultural competency and empathy did harm me nonetheless.

At the time, the cultural aloofness that I often encountered from certain educators felt brutal and cruel, but in hindsight I realize they were conditioned to think that way. Identity is a complicated thing. It is extremely nuanced. To be subject to people who are unaware of where you come from, your culture, or your life circumstances but who try to define your identity or demand your conformity based on their assumption of who they think you are can be a dangerous endeavor. The impact that this practice has on us personally can change the course of our lives forever, and the impact that it has on us socially can change how we view the world for good or bad.

Socialization, then, is part and parcel with schooling. The word *socialize* is a verb, and its meaning extends beyond participating in social activities; to socialize also means to make someone behave in ways that are suitable for society.

What did it mean, then, to be prepared by an education system that saw me as it wanted to see me, only to be equipped for a society that was not equipped for me? The answer to that question gives us the greatest opportunity to tell the truth: we are not as self-aware as we think we are. Critical self-awareness is the ability to be aware of ourselves—our actions, thoughts, and emotions—to see how we, through our actions and thoughts, contribute to further the conflicts and/or collapses in society.

We've all been shaped by a social reality that picks winners and losers before they ever get into the game. In addition, "our society has socialized us to not raise critical questions" about the impediments that are perpetuated in our education system and other social institutions. Dorinda Carter Andrews highlighted this in her TEDxLansingED talk when she said, "One of the things that I think prevents us from closing what are actually access and opportunity gaps is our inability to name issues of power as fundamental to the racial and cultural divide in this country."

Her statement underscores the need for courageous conversations regarding how educators are socialized and how their racial identities impact how we educate our children. What if we all questioned our positionality in society and our relationship to systemic and institutional power? That's what critical consciousness does. Critical consciousness as a social philosophy was developed in 1970 by Paulo Freire, a Brazilian educator. His work *Pedagogy of the Oppressed* explored this idea. Freire wanted to "liberate the masses from systematic inequity maintained and perpetuated by process, practices, and outcomes from interdependent systems and institutions." He taught that if people are unaware of inequalities and the imbalance of power and do not resist the status quo, then society will have remnants of those inequalities in its culture and institutions. In his mind this would result in what he called "residual inequity in perpetuity."

As I sat in Mr. Harris's office, what I didn't know then was that he was taking critical action. With striking vulnerability, he shared with me that day that he often felt complicit in watching kids fall through the cracks in education. He felt powerless to act—he was just an athletic director—until he developed the critical mindset to morally reject systemic issues. In his words, "If you see something wrong in society, you are morally obligated to act to fix it."

Critical consciousness enables a heightened awareness of the world and the power structures that shape it. It also allows us to see our real ability to change the inequitable aspects that are in it. No one is truly powerless.

But of course this begs the question, Can public education in its current form be a revolutionary agent for change? Or must it be an agent only of repeating the same patterns that have brought us to the difficulties and inequities of our present day?

Thomas Aquinas observed, "Whatever is received into anything must be received according to the condition of the receiver." This insight simply means that we don't see things as they are; we see things as *we* are. To a large degree, we choose what we believe. If we believe that our system of education can be an agent of revolutionary change, then it will be. Conversely, if we believe that inequality and inequity in education are too big of a problem to solve, then we will never solve it.

To advocate through a critical-consciousness framework is an inspiring, strengths-based, problem-solving approach that empowers and strengthens engagement, helping to address inequality and transcend inequity. What if every student, parent, and educator operated from that framework of belief—*that they could make a difference?* We would truly see ourselves and one another. Our schools and, more importantly, the *outcomes* that our schools produce, especially for marginalized students, would look completely different.

In that room, Mr. Harris and Mrs. Robinson were advocating for me because they saw themselves clearly. They saw the real role they played, even if often unrecognized or ignored, in unlocking student potential. They believed—which made it possible for them to see all of me and the capacity I had. They were working as if my identity and achievement were inextricably linked, in the tacit understanding that underserved students are the ones that are impacted the most negatively if they don't have educators who can go a little farther to help them navigate race, culture, and their social surroundings.

I'm not sure if we can leave the task of helping develop positive cultural and ethnic identity in students to public schooling. That may be asking too much of our school system. But I am certain that the adults whom students encounter in school should be able and willing to help—to pass on the proficiency and acquired immunities earned by previous generations to build resilience against a mixture of intellectual and social ills. Institutional and cultural racism are such ills. As adults we are obligated not to transmit our social diseases to the next generation but to provide them with the antidotes in case the old social ills resurface.

Looking back today, with my experiences as a community leader and advocate for education, I can see that as a student of color, I was victimized by educators. That may sound extreme or unfair, and surely it was largely unintentional. But that doesn't diminish the impact. The truth is that the lived experiences in my schooling negatively influenced how I came to see myself. Encounters in my community traumatized me at an early age. From kindergarten, I had to fight off prejudice and racial tropes from adults in school. In my neighborhood, I had to contend with acting like I didn't care about school while longing to show my love for education, often concealing those feelings for my own safety. Fitting in was a survival tactic. I had to figure out who I was when my family system was altered by the death of my father. Without his presence, I was left looking at the models of manhood I had in my orbit, which were mostly hustlers.

The combination of adversities for me was like an oil spill in the ocean, floating on the surface of my emotions. Negativity on top of identity formation just doesn't mix. Trauma of any kind makes it hard to articulate who you are or speak about your ambitions out loud. I had been traumatized by the community I grew up in by the time I got to middle school, and you can't just shake that off. The lack of critical consciousness and cultural competence in the adults that I interacted within the majority of social institutions was a daily reminder of how inequities are baked into the societal cake.

"I treat all students the same."

I heard some version of this a thousand times. Many educators would say this on the first day of class or use another phrase that rang even hollower: "I don't see color."

You don't see color? Then how will you see *me*? Racial identity is a key component of one's overall identity. It cannot be overlooked or undermined. Equality, as such, is not equity. Even if race is never mentioned in a classroom, the intimation is that certain cultural characteristics and differences are often seen as inferior and others superior. Students with vastly different life experiences, traditions, academic readiness, and strengths don't need to be treated equally; they need equity. As the common analogy says and I mentioned earlier, equality is when everyone gets a pair of shoes, but equity is when everyone gets a pair of shoes that fit. School never fit for me, and the victimization was that I had to go through it wearing the unselfconsciously small assumptions of adults.

To move forward, I had to tell myself the following: *I will take criticism, and I will take opposition. But society can keep its negativity.*

I was seventeen years old and had never tied a tie before. I made all-county my senior year, and they held an awards ceremony that required wearing a real tie that they gave out to every awardee. All my ties were clip-ons.

Attempt after attempt to tie a knot failed. Finally, I punched a hole in the drywall out of total frustration. As I looked at the dark gap broken in the wall, my knuckles stinging, tears rolled down my cheeks like rocks. It was a *tie*. How could a little thing be so heavy? I felt the fatigue of fighting alone. I felt regret. The shadow of guilt and remorse for what I'd done on the streets filled the bathroom. I was left alone with my history and the feeling of not measuring up. I felt completely ridiculous. Isolated.

"Sometimes you have to be a lion so you can be the lamb you really are." Comedian Dave Chappelle said that his mother told him this when he was a kid, and that's what life felt like for me. I became this lionhearted person only to defend the lamb that was on the inside. Most of the time I was just scared. Now the thought of going to college terrified me even more. I was about to graduate high school, and I had some real soul-searching to do. I massaged my fist and wondered why for so long it had become easier and easier for me to fly off the handle. My disguise had been the bad-boy athlete. That thing was working. But who was I going to be now? There was still a little boy inside.

I felt shame because I was so angry. I didn't know how to ask for help or that it was even okay to do so. It's not that there weren't any men who could have shown me how to tie a tie or do other things, but I just never trusted anybody enough to say, "I don't know how." Trying to tie that knot almost broke me because it was a reminder of how many times I was stuck there by myself, learning on my own.

I decided that I would stay there until I could tie it. There was something about the mirror that made me look at myself. The real me. Not my projection of a bad boy or label of star athlete. Just *Michael*. I wanted to do it for him. I didn't want him to be abandoned in that moment. I stared at myself until I tied that knot. After the awards ceremony, Mr. Harris came over to tell me to let go of all that happened and be open to the new possibilities ahead. Mrs. Robinson assisted me in filling out my college applications. Mr. Harris set up all my college visits, but it was so late in the game that I still had trouble unraveling from the unexamined assumptions that had cloaked my identity for years.

I was terrified of stepping out into the unknown.

But I had to.

CHAPTER SIX

Crash

Turn your wounds into wisdom. You will be wounded
many times in your life. You'll make mistakes.

—OPRAH WINFREY

After visiting a variety of colleges and viewing the scholarship offers to a host of schools, I made my choice. I
graduated in May 1992 and entered my freshman year a few
months later.

If it weren't for two adults in my high school that believed
in my ability to achieve success in college and beyond, I would
have continued to be influenced by the poorly conceptual-
ized, negative data points that are typical assumptions of a
Black male. Most of the focus during my high school education centered on avoiding delinquency and getting a good job
rather than preparing me for college.

Although I was a college-bound athlete, there was still a deficit narrative synonymous with my skin color. Such narratives came from adults—not just ones I encountered at school but in general. It seemed that many educators I encountered as a young man assumed that I wasn't motivated to learn. But that perception was completely wrong. I was intelligent and loved learning. What dampened that motivation, almost to the point of extinguishing it, were misplaced assessments about me, starting with those first stinging words from Miss Battle. There are many barriers to postsecondary education for Black students. But there is an overwhelming desire among them to be educated at the highest level.

Many Black students lack the opportunities needed to enter and excel in college even before they graduate from high school. Data shows that Black students have less access to the full variety of math and science courses needed for college admission. Contrary to the widely held belief that racial inequalities in education are the product of student disengagement, according to a research report entitled *A Seat at the Table,* presented by the United Negro College Fund, Black youth stated that academic achievement was *their top priority* despite the barriers they face.

Without equity-minded practice there can be no disruption of deficit narratives. Deficit thought is embedded in a blame-the-victim mentality that implies that individuals are accountable for their circumstances and fails to recognize that they exist inside systemic environments that inflict damage without accountability. For all my challenges, I was neither a problem to be solved nor a broken individual to be fixed. I was a young Black male who wanted to learn.

Being systemically characterized as hopeless is like having a wound that never heals. I honestly believed that I would not graduate high school, that I would end up in jail, and, even worse, that my life would be taken by violence. If I was going to succeed in college, I would have to contend with the negative typecasting that I heard so often.

We *think* we know the facts that shape our biases, but it's never that simple. Everybody carries bias. It's part of being human. And growing beyond our biases is part of work we all need to do as members of society. These biases commonly show up implicitly—not as brash or shocking actions or opinions but as much more palatable or "reasonable" viewpoints. Those implicit associations reside in our subconscious minds. They produce attitudes and feelings that support stereotypes that affect our understanding of individuals, people groups, and even ourselves. They develop over a lifetime, informed by not only direct but also indirect messaging. But we can't allow our biases to go unchecked, because repeating false or inaccurate statements causes more wounds than we can imagine.

When we hear partial or even false statistics—like the "fact" that "there are more Black males in a cell than there are in college" or that "overwhelmingly, Black fathers are absent"—we not only take them as truth, but we also take them a step farther, allowing them to shift our expectations. Absence among Black dads is not the norm. Black fathers are very likely to live with their kids, although there are exceptions. A 2006–2010 CDC study estimated that about 2.5 million Black dads were living with their children, and about 1.7 million were living away from them; the latter doesn't mean that these dads were not involved in their children's lives. When it comes to Black men in prison versus Black men in college, it depends on what year you pull the data from. In the US in 2013, for example, more than 1.4 million Black males were enrolled in a degree-granting institution, compared with about 746,000 Black males incarcerated that same year.

As Jenée Desmond-Harris pointed out, "Numbers aside, the college vs. prison comparison is problematic on its face. Men (of all races) can be incarcerated at any point in their lives for any length of time, while enrollment in college typically happens during a narrow age range and a short time span. So contrasting the two experiences is an apples-to-oranges exercise." In no way am I trying to undermine the importance of understanding the problem of mass incarceration, the disparate systems of confinement, and the need to end both, which has been notably stated by Michelle Alexander in *The New Jim Crow*. We really do have a major problem when 38 percent of the prison population is Black yet

Black people represent only 13 percent of the total population in America.

Mass incarceration impacts millions of people, but it is the collateral consequences that do the most damage for Black people who have been incarcerated and even for those who have not. The stigma of criminality has become associated with being Black and, in particular, being a Black male. When we overestimate data, we underestimate potential. Overestimations like the ones I mentioned earlier perpetuate myths that are easier to believe because of the biases that are already in our brains.

Unchecked bias is a thief that prohibits us from seeing what is right in front of our eyes and steals our chance to learn from one another. The danger of unchecked bias is that it cloaks the individual and daggers the opportunity to change our perceptions and deeply held beliefs.

I wanted to succeed in college more than anything, but the wounds that I had already suffered never properly healed before the next calamity struck. Not even halfway through my first semester of college, we had a short weekend break, so I decided to go home. I missed everybody and could admit that I was a little homesick. The start of school had been great. I was working out with the basketball team, scrimmaging, and getting to know my teammates. I knew I had a great chance to start, and as a true freshman that would have been something.

When I reconnected with all my friends, instead of throwing me a party, they decided we should go to a local club. We partied all night. It was great to be back in B-more, to hear the unique club music that hits you in the chest like the bass is inside you. The night passed, and the dawn came, finding us still having a great time. After getting some breakfast, all of us wanted to go to an amusement park, and since it was a few hours away, we ended up driving there straight from the breakfast spot. It was 5 a.m. We figured if we left then, we would make it to the park right when it opened. It sounded like a good idea.

One of the vehicles we took was a red, two-seat sports car. I hopped in that one. As we took off, I leaned my seat back all the way and extended my legs. My seat belt didn't move, so it remained stretched out inches above me. The stillness of the early morning coupled with the darkness outside made my eyelids heavy. The driver was tired, too, but (thankfully) neither of us were intoxicated. I decided to get some sleep before the fun continued.

Boom.

I woke up to a loud scraping sound and looked out to see that we were hitting the guardrail along the highway. The car was moving so fast—shooting sparks and smoke blurred my vision—and when I peered over to my friend, I saw him waking up from having fallen asleep, trying to get control of the vehicle. It was too late.

Seconds. That's all it took. But each felt like eternity.

The sports car slid off the road and struck a rock embankment. Our momentum glanced us off, sending us spinning across the highway and head-on into the opposite guardrail. The hood of the car slid underneath the guardrail while the rest bashed against the metal. The metal around the windshield crumpled like a can, the glass shattering to dust. The driver had an airbag, but I did not. I went forcefully forward in the collision as the seat belt shredded like tissue paper across my chest. While my lower right leg remained pinned below the dashboard, my upper torso went through the opening in the windshield.

When I woke up, I was in the hospital. I found myself strapped to a board on a gurney, unable to feel my legs. I wondered if I was completely paralyzed. I couldn't see my leg, but I knew it was bad simply because of the way they had me strapped down. The driver had suffered only some bumps and bruises—the airbag saved him from serious injury.

Soon, the doctor walked in and told me what in my heart I already knew. I had crushed my right leg entirely. I had a shattered kneecap, plus a broken tibia, a broken fibula, three broken toes, and a snapped Achilles tendon.

"You won't be able to play basketball again," the doctor told me. "It's not even likely you'll walk again."

Those words. Their reality covered my hospital room,

darker than midnight in December. I knew it immediately. My hoop dreams had ended. In that single moment, my future, my purpose, and my potential all seemed to have been crushed along with my leg. My eyes watered, but nothing came down my cheeks. Sometimes the loudest pain is held in silent tears.

If the doctor was telling me I might not even *walk* again, then I definitely wouldn't be playing basketball. Ever.

So, who am I now if I can't hoop? Who am I if I can't run? What am I supposed to do now?

Sounds strange that I would have such questions rolling around in my medicated, foggy brain, but it's how I dealt with the shock. The news from the doctor was more painful than my injuries. It felt like the ground was falling out from under me. Then came the fear.

Then came the old, familiar fury.

Bitterness followed after the first wave of fear crashed down and carried a question in its wake: *Where is God?*

I tried. I tried to think rationally. I tried to have optimism, but the compounding wounds of words, expectations, and calamity after calamity would not allow it. I suppose that is the nature of a crisis. It doesn't discriminate, and it tries to take away the light so you believe that the darkness is real. When you're in the dark and when you are desperate, you'll believe anything.

I will never walk again?

The question hit me so hard I lost my breath. I could see my chances slipping away.

To get my nerves together and stop my mind from racing, I imagined that I could hear my father's voice. In my mind I could hear him preaching with his raspy booming sound; it silenced the waves of fear that were crashing over my head: *"We always have hope in the midst of life's havoc. We always have an advocate even when we feel alone. We always have a destination prepared for us even if all we see are plans destroyed."* I could hear Dad preaching, *"Surely I know the plans I have for you, says the* LORD, *plans for your welfare and not for harm, to give you a future with hope."*

As I began a long road to recovery in the hospital, I tried to believe it. I tried to believe that God had plans for me, for all of this. They tried to give me Percocet and other medication for my pain, but I refused it all. I didn't want to be addicted to anything. I decided to live through the pain—I already had enough inner wounds, and it felt honest, somehow, to let my body hurt too.

When I got back home, my head coach told me to stay there since there was no need for me to try to get back to campus. But I wanted to go back given that my options for anything positive to happen were extremely limited at home. After calling my professors—who already knew my situation—I ended up going back for the spring semester. I arrived on campus disappointed and totally unprepared to be a college student instead of a student athlete.

That semester, I sat in my dorm most days with my leg in a large cast—drinking and smoking blunts. I could not cope. Every day that I woke up, I wished that it was all just a nightmare. I became hopelessly behind in my schoolwork. It all began to disintegrate as reality sunk in. This was not a dream. It was real. The life I had briefly enjoyed was over. I felt powerless, useless, and insignificant. After putting me on academic probation, the school decided to withdraw my scholarship and (nicely) uninvited me to stay.

I returned home. I felt like a complete failure. I had spent only three months on campus, if you combined both semesters, and then it was over. Just like that. The fear of being another statistic, an uneducated Black male, was a troubling scenario for me. The echo from years of harsh words reverberated in my head. Weaponized thoughts injured my ability to believe for better. In my mind, I was doomed, fixed to a permanent status of less than.

But instead of seeing this as a setback, I saw it as defeat. I had been told the majority of my life that I could not achieve success. When individuals are told from childhood and beyond what they can or cannot be, their future will ultimately be affected.

Nothing chips away at purpose like the soft bigotry of low expectations. If failure is all that is expected of us, then failure becomes seemingly insurmountable and waiting to trounce us at every turn. What we do habitually will always triumph over what happens occasionally. Fear and anger were my emotional habits. Nothing could be reordered in my life with that type of mental orientation. I had no practice with living in paradox, with seeing wins and losses coexisting together. It was always win-lose and never win-win. The best I could do was hope that I would fall into the hands of mercy. But how could I trust that now? I decided that I would rather control the outcome. And with that decision, some of my greatest mistakes in life began.

Taking control of your life sounds practical. Kids are told it's the "adult" thing to do. One last time, I closed my eyes to see if I could hear my father preaching. The sound was infinitesimal. *"Trust in the* LORD *with all your heart, and do not rely on your own insight. In all your ways acknowledge him, and he will make straight your paths."* Then it was gone. I was too wounded to hear wisdom. I was fragile. I was defensive. Standing on one leg, I could see the predictable patterns of struggle like waves on sand.

I saw what I had to do. Control is a seductive complement to pain.

My future is in my hands. I'm going to choose to become what I feared the most.

Like a serpent lying still in the weeds, the street waited for me. I still knew all the hustlers and big-time players. They all knew me as Little Mike, everybody's little brother. They all looked out for me. Many of them wanted me to aspire to be better than they were. When I was a kid, they would say comments like "You don't need to be out here. Stick with basketball. This ain't your world."

And they were right. Compared to some of the guys I knew, it was completely evident to me that I didn't belong there. I was from the hood, but I was not hood. You can't dabble in the street; dabblers lose their lives in that game. All I could do was think about the real criminals that I knew growing up. Those guys were the real deal. These were the type of men who were convinced that the only world they could be great in was the underworld.

This was their way of life. It wasn't mine. Yet.

Back in high school, I had tried to work for a guy named Left. He was a phenomenal left-handed basketball player. I met him playing ball in the summer leagues and different big street games. That was the subculture back then: playing a big street game for money. Guys would put up thousands of dollars in some of those games. Left was the quintessential cautionary tale. He was a man with more talent in his pinkie than the majority of people who "made it." He could have been a household name, a hero. Instead, in the end, Left was murdered at a barbershop. His criminal drug enterprise stretched from Virginia to Philadelphia. He owned a few businesses, and in terms of sheer leadership talent, he more than likely could have run any Fortune 500 company. I begged him to let me work for him, but he always said no.

"This is short money," he would say. "There is no 401(k) for drug dealers."

Left never let me do it.

"No, man. You're gonna be great. This ain't for you, so stay away."

Thinking back through all the people I saw rise and fall gave me a brief moment of pause. Trying for anything I could, I took a job that summer at a basketball camp as a counselor. My leg was still in an Aircast boot, and I still walked around on crutches. It had seemed like a good idea, but seeing the kids run up and down the court the first day of camp didn't inspire me; it triggered me.

That same week, a few friends wanted me to go out with them one evening in hopes of making me feel better. They dragged me away to our favorite club in the city. I ran into one of my old high school teammates. We sat in the VIP room drinking and talking, and I learned that he had a similar story to mine. He went to college, too, but left after the first semester for various reasons. I asked him a question that would prove to be life-altering for me.

"So, what are you doing for money?"

He laughed, then leaned over to whisper in my ear, "Whatever I have to do."

It was the answer I had been rehearsing in my head and

the one I think I was hoping to hear. My story was already tragic. I was in too much pain to wait for it to get better. Besides, now I was just the average Black guy walking down the block. I had the same story and the same narrative as so many others according to society. I could have a shot only at mediocre jobs. I was a college dropout, a once-upon-a-time hoop phenom with a busted leg. So I figured I had one more shot with a few seconds left on the clock, and I took it.

I had some money to invest. So two days after meeting with my friend, I became his partner, and we purchased our first kilo of cocaine.

CHAPTER SEVEN

Short Money

Wherever purpose is not known, abuse is inevitable.
—MYLES MUNROE

My first major drug deal was not as exhilarating as I thought it would be. It was an uneventful, nonchalant transaction. No guns, no drama. But I knew from that point on I would be at war with myself. It was a civil war between my worst self and my better angels, between doing what was right and doing what was easy, between my selfish interests and what was best for my community. I was losing myself to the tyranny of the immediate. With every corner I took over, I could hear the faint whispers of my ancestors, but the only word I could make out from the ambient echo was *betrayer.* Deep down, I knew I was betraying the line of heroes and martyrs my grandmother and my parents had so often talked about: civil rights icons like Rosa Parks and Fannie Lou Hamer and great champions like Arthur Ashe and Muhammad Ali.

I had no excuse. Growing up, my family often talked about the struggles and triumphs of Black people. Their stories were part of me. Rosa Parks was arrested for not giving up her seat on a bus to a White person in the Jim Crow South. Fannie Lou Hamer was a champion for voters' rights and stood up singing "This Little Light of Mine" while the driver of the bus who transported them to vote was arrested. She was later arrested and beaten for helping to organize students to participate in a sit-in at a Whites-only lunch counter. Women and men bled and died for the freedoms that I was enjoying, yet here I stood. Doing . . . *this.*

Was it as simple as my choices, or did my defiance stem from tasting the sour grapes of the historic vine that now had my teeth on edge?

Only the "mystic chords of memory" that stretch from heroes to villains and from martyrs to monsters can harmonize our understanding. It wasn't just my choices at work; it was much more complex than that.

We have a long history of waging war with ourselves.

The year 1865 marked the culmination of the Civil War and the adoption of the Thirteenth Amendment.

It also triggered the nation's first prison boom when the number of black Americans arrested and incarcerated surged. This was the result of state legislatures reacting to two powerful social forces: first, public anxiety and fear about crime stemming from newly freed black Americans; and second, economic depression resulting from the war and the loss of a free supply of labor. State and local leaders in the South used the criminal justice system to both pacify the public's fear and bolster the depressed economy. All across the South, Black Codes were passed that outlawed behaviors common to black people, such as "walking without a purpose."

Newly freed slaves, predominately Black males, were being arrested for simply walking down the street or settling on public land.

For generations, Black men were seen as monsters and brutes, or they had to become martyrs for the cause of the full promise professed in the Declaration of Independence. From post-Reconstruction to present day, we are still calling young Black males thugs just because of their physical size or loud voices. We do it when we see them standing on corners and walking down streets, without knowing anything about them. Failing to recognize the historical link between race and class, culture and opportunity, marginalizes our understanding of our roles in people's choices.

You cannot call me a threat my entire life and not expect me to become one.

I became a rebel with no cause except my anger. But in spite of it all, I could not escape the love of my mother. I sat in the corner of the church sanctuary on Sunday mornings, even though it was the last place I wanted to be. Nevertheless, I had promised her that I would attend church. My attitude toward faith had not changed since my father's funeral. If anything, my hatred toward God had grown and my apathy for religion had become cemented. I came for my mother's sake, but that Sunday morning, I realized just what a great thing attending service regularly could be.

Church was a good cover.

Kids around my neighborhood used to call me "church boy." They meant it as an insult, but now it would become my disguise. I faithfully attended services, sitting in the front row and singing. I always enjoyed the music, but I hated the memories of Sunday mornings. Every week I stood a few feet away from where my father's body had rested. I felt numb. There were authentic moments where I could feel God's power, where I could sense His Spirit in the sanctuary, but I didn't want to have anything to do with that.

Nor did I want to have anything to do with approaching the drug game like the character of Nino Brown in *New Jack*

City. There were no kingpins living in palaces, not in real life. I thought it would be best to have another cover for my real "work," so I took a job as a grill cook at a local sports pub. I worked the lunch shift, four or five hours each day. This, of course, was just to keep things seeming on the up-and-up, to show people where the money was coming from. The owner of the pub was a former professional football player. His son and I had played on the same all-star basketball team, and he hired me on sight. It was a good gig for the goals I had.

My partner and I started out small, but my brain has always had a problem with small. I wanted to figure out how we could scale what we were doing. I thought it was ironic that I could get a student loan for a hundred thousand but I couldn't get a business loan for ten thousand. From my vantage point, this was the only opportunity I had left.

My goal was to make 250K and get out.

The first kilo we bought we flipped several times, making a tidy profit, but we didn't have the structure to do anything larger. We needed a strategy, more people, and more cash. Then, provided we got those things in place, we needed to execute. We thought about it all in a very businesslike manner, like venture capitalists or CEOs. Blue tops and good business were our brand essence. The tops that went on the crack valves were color coded per region. We created our own competition, making it appear that other competitors were in the space. Whether the tops were blue, green, red, or yellow, they were all ours. Blue tops signaled the best quality.

We worked hard and were treated with respect. It was "good business." After all, we were thinkers, not thugs.

The goal? Dominate the crack market. Since everyone else was interested in copping dope, no one was filling the niche for a drug that brought you up instead of taking you down. We needed to find a strategic partner to launder our money until we could accomplish the goal of being vertically integrated. We put more guys on the street—mostly young teens who just wanted sneaker money, just like I did when I was their age.

As young men we think the answer to life is money; more money means our problems will go away. Money answers all things, but there is a pedagogy to purpose, a method and a practice for teaching. If you tell me to go to school but it has no meaning, then what's the outcome? If schooling centers on achievement that will never earn me an elite position in life, then it offers no purpose. My environment taught me that if you had money, you had power. School didn't offer purpose, and neither did we. We just offered money.

This is how we recruited young teens. I knew we had an opportunity with them, because in their classrooms they had been seen more for their behavior than for their brilliance. I expected them to be as alienated and frustrated as I had been in their shoes. For them, instruction was centered on the teacher and not the student. Instinctively when we know something is not real, we reject the notion of false generosity. The subjects in school are separated from the real world, and the students are then separated from the subjects, creating sterile learning environments in an unsanitary world. The street involved learning by doing in an atmosphere of social constructivism. Your peers and the people you encountered gave instant feedback, while the problems you faced were how scholarship happened. It wasn't authoritarian; it was authentic. We offered the carrot to young people, not the stick. We knew their families, helped them get groceries, and paid some of their bills.

The pedagogy of poverty is cruel, and it doesn't work.

In the majority of urban schools that we recruited from, the instructional practices were skewed more toward dumping information and enforcing behavior than toward providing opportunities for students to raise questions, make sense of the environment, and address challenges in their families and beyond. This is the pedagogy of poverty. Just because kids are poor or come from a poor environment doesn't mean they need to be taught how to behave. It means they need someone to validate their beliefs that there is a better life and that education is the right path to it. That's what these young men were looking for: *How can I make life better for me and my family?*

In some distorted way we thought we were helping them achieve that. But the deeper we got into it, the more it became clear that we were doing more harm than good. Instead of trying to walk away, we stepped further into the darkness, hoping that we could make something good out of it.

Access to capital was our greatest hurdle. We had two options: steal or partner. We decided on the second of those options, partnering with a heroin dealer. We would provide our "girl" cocaine to complement his "boy" heroin. In return he offered protection and cash for equity in our business. The beauty of our business plan was that none of our contractors directly knew whom they were working for. In an underground economy, anonymity is a best practice.

Ironically, there are fewer barriers to entry in the underworld than in legitimate business. Corner liquor stores and blight were ubiquitous. There was no need to invest in customer acquisition—that was already done for us. All we had to do was position our product next to pain and we could practically operate our "shop" in the open air.

It doesn't matter where you come from or the color of your skin or the size of your bank account—we all have pain. Everyone experiences it uniquely, but that meant everybody came to us to self-medicate for that unique pain. Our customer base was broad, multiracial, and diverse in socioeconomic status, and that was just on the supply side. I saw a White businessman hand over the keys to his Corvette for a few thousand dollars' worth of cocaine. I witnessed professionals purchasing crack on the way to their offices. Mothers. Fathers.

The person that gave me the deepest understanding of

addiction—and genuine feelings of regret for what I was doing—was Grace. She was a registered nurse at a prestigious hospital who happened to live in the same suburb as my mom. She would pass our spot during her morning commute. Grace was beautiful. Like, *Halle Berry* beautiful. Until suddenly, she wasn't. Without notice she suddenly deteriorated, becoming a shell of herself. Rarely did I interact with any customers, but one day Grace came up to me, begging for a dime valve of crack.

It was my turn to inspect the blocks. When she started speaking, I didn't notice her and just said, "I'll be with you in a minute." Then she said my name. I recognized her voice and turned, shocked at what she had become. She must have lost thirty pounds. Her face was sunken; her eyes were bright, sick, and very hungry; her cheek bones protruded from her face.

"Grace?"

"Stop playing," she said.

I offered her a ride home since we both lived in the same suburb. I had to know what happened. "Why are you on drugs?" I asked as we drove.

Without hesitating, with her head held high, she said one of the most insightful things I had ever heard: "We are all on something. We are all addicted to something."

I didn't need the backstory after that. Of course. Addiction is addiction. It has multiple expressions, but the object of dependency can be just about anything. Our sickness was the

same. She used a substance, and I used power. She was buying; I was selling. That was the only difference. I dropped her
off and drove away, watching her nervously stride off . . . toward what?

The suburbs offered no more shelter from substance abuse
than the city did. People were getting high out there, too, but
the market was more wholesale. White boys bought 8 balls
like they were dime bags. Weed was popular as well. But as
the weeks passed, I couldn't shake what Grace said. I wondered how long I could keep this up. I was beginning to feel
like a thief of lives.

I had become addicted to the power of selling drugs, but I
could not ignore the damage. My first thoughts of getting out
came from an old memory. When I was in high school, one of
my good friends was a guy named Darnell. He had grown up
in a similar environment as I did, and like me he had a lot of
trauma. We smoked a lot of weed together.

Once while we were in his house, Darnell took a bag of
weed out and placed it on the kitchen table. I assumed we
were alone, so when I heard the shuffling of feet and realized
his mother was home as well, I froze, trying to figure out a
way to hide the bud before she could see it.

She's going to kill us, I thought in terror. Why was Darnell
acting so *oblivious*?

His mother walked up to the table before I could act. I
waited for her to start yelling at us, but instead, she sat down
and began to smoke with us.

For some reason, that encounter haunted me. When I met Darnell at thirteen, his dad was in prison for drug trafficking. His mother had done a stretch too. Recalling the image of his mother smoking weed with him was, strangely enough, the beginning of a change for me. Would that be the legacy I'd leave my kids? I had no children but knew that when and if I did, I could not let them inherit my trauma. Dark moments somehow make our eyes see. Between the encounter with Grace and the memory of Darnell's mom surrounded by that acrid smoke, I started to dream of going legit.

But power is a hard thing to let go of. Just as I was trying to get out, an opportunity was presented to us. Not just any opportunity but one of the *big* ones. It had major risk, but the rewards were too massive not to take the chance. "Why don't you guys come rock out on the east side?" The heroin dealer we were in business with offered us a new spot that was perfect for our operation. We would have two row homes side by side to work from, along with an abandoned school building across the street. At the top of the corner was a liquor store and carryout. At the other end of the block was a very small street that looked like a dead end. We could bag, stash, and distribute without worry. The danger? We were not from the east side. If it went bad, blood would be spilled. A lot of it. But we were all in agreement: the risk was worth the reward.

We called our new venture Schoolhouse Rocks. Pablo

Escobar we were not, but our little enterprise was getting it done. Not only did we sell crack, but we also had a chop shop for stolen cars, multiple locations for distribution and retail, and a handful of employees and contractors. Our crew consisted of around twenty guys, managed by four heads. Playboy ran our corners. He earned that nickname on account of his good hair. He was a pretty boy with something to prove, but we were willing to overlook that since he had a lot of connections on the east side. Skip was our muscle. At six feet and 260 pounds, he was like a giant bowling ball. Also like a bowling ball, he was reckless, willing to roll right through anything. He was dangerous. He was also the person you needed in a sticky situation. T and I were the founding partners, so we oversaw everything. And just like that, we had scaled up. I was defining myself for myself. No one was going to tell me who I was.

Or at least, that's what I told myself.

Everything was moving too fast. In just one year of my life, the idea of making a little money turned into something extremely serious. My little side ventures were getting out of control, eventually crossing a boundary I had wanted to avoid—federal crime. My firm, early policy of knowing the rules before you broke them had fallen by the wayside.

Worse, people were taking notice, and I was beginning to

believe the hype about me. Arrogance is kin to ignorance. Winning this way quickly tempts you to believe you are invincible, as if you're made of Teflon and impervious to harm.

It took just one altercation to change my mind. The entire time we were in operation, I had no violent situations until one day when a particular girl walked past me. She was beautiful, and I did what all young men did in the hood—I shot my shot. Who would have thought that a few kind words were enough to start a would-be war?

I hadn't seen her boyfriend in the car. He hopped out, and we exchanged a few words . . . but I still got her number. Turned out, though, that the boyfriend wasn't a nobody. He was a legend in his neighborhood, just returning home from a ten-year stretch in jail. Moments later I noticed something strange. The block had cleared. No one was walking or sitting on stoops. Activity in the schoolhouse had slowed dramatically. It was too quiet. Skip said, "Something's up." Not seconds after he spoke, we saw what seemed like fifty guys walking toward us with bats, guns, and knives. It was the boyfriend with his crew coming to deal with me for speaking to his girl.

Our first instinct was to grab our straps, but then Playboy spoke up. "Yo, I know him." We didn't run. Outnumbered— and we didn't run. I should've been terrified, but somehow I wasn't. Playboy and the boyfriend had done time together. The beef was squashed with a handshake.

The insanity of pride progressively makes your spirit obnoxious. Your whole makeup changes—the way you talk to people, the way you carry yourself. I was obtuse toward death because I didn't care about life. I flaunted my apathy like a Rolex after the incident. Providence had protected me despite my arrogance and indifference. But as the proverb says, "Pride goes before destruction, and a haughty spirit before a fall."

In the movies or on television, the beginning of the end would have come from a competing drug lord or a snitch or a drug deal gone bad, but for me, my whole elaborate enterprise started crashing down after I got a traffic ticket. That's right: *a traffic ticket.*

One day I got pulled over for running a stop sign. *Not a problem,* I thought. We never used our real names, and we had many fake IDs. That night I had been drinking and didn't have any ID on me. So I gave the police officer a name of a friend that I knew would check out. The officer gave me the ticket for running the stop sign and driving without a license, and I went on my way.

A few weeks later, I received a call from my friend. "Hey, man. My dad is really angry."

It turns out that his father had received my traffic ticket in the mail and asked him about it, assuming it belonged to his son. After my friend said it wasn't his, they discovered that I had falsified my name. I apologized to him and said I'd make it right.

"Tell your dad I'll go to court and settle the matter. I'll pay the ticket."

"My dad doesn't believe you're going," he said.

"Watch me. I'm gonna go."

When the court date came, sure enough, I walked into that courtroom and gave them my name. I explained what happened and paid the fine. I assumed that would be the end of things. What I didn't know was that my name was already in the system. They had a warrant out for my arrest. The Feds had been watching us—not for narcotics but for using the names of recently deceased people to acquire credit cards. We either sold the cards or charged them up and sold off the goods. As the clerk was telling me to wait, I saw the anxiety in her eyes, looked for the door, and ran.

The same day, a kid running from narc cops ran into our stash house. This was a house we owned. We allowed one of our customers to live there, and we operated out of the space. At the time, we had around $50,000 in cash and three to four kilos of cocaine inside. The kid surprised Playboy, who thought someone was coming in to rob us. Playboy started shooting at the guys following the kid. He ended up shooting a cop and also got shot himself.

When the shooting happened, I was on my way to the stash house after leaving my job at the pub. I had money hidden at my job and near the stash house. I needed as much cash as I could get my hands on. My partner called me.

"Hey man, don't come down," T told me. "We got raided."

"What?"

"Yeah, we got raided. We need to lay low."

At the time he didn't know that Playboy had been shot.

"Where are you?" I asked.

"I'm gonna head out of town," T said.

"I'm out too," I replied.

I grabbed some clothes, threw them in my car, and took off as quickly as I could. I made it to Richmond, Virginia, in three hours. There, I got a hotel room and waited. I learned that Playboy was shot, so we decided we needed to stay low a little longer so we could figure out who was coming at us and why.

The next day, I learned that Skip was dead after being shot. All hell was breaking loose, and I didn't know the full details, but I knew enough to be convinced I needed to get far away from Baltimore.

Someone's trying to kill us, I thought. I imagined that it might be the boyfriend coming back or some other crew trying to take us out but that it was all coincidence or karma.

The heroin dealer we were in business with had been under surveillance for months. The traffic ticket and the kid being chased by the narcs set off a series of events that ultimately resulted in our downfall. As soon as Playboy traded bullets with the cops, the guys watching us because of the heroin dealer had to give up their cover. Federal officers told the narc cops that they were surveilling us for fraud, believing that it was all under the umbrella of the heroin dealer's operation. Coincidentally, a drug crew was taken down because of a traffic ticket and some kid we didn't know who had five dollars' worth of crack on him.

Schoolhouse Rocks shut down. It was over.

Skip being shot and killed had nothing to do with the Feds or the narc cops. Our boy ended up getting shot over some girl. It was devastating to lose him, and I wanted to go as far south as I could until I could think things through. That's when my mother called me.

"I want to have breakfast with you," she said.

"Mom, I can't. I gotta go."

"No, Michael," she said in a stern voice. "Federal officers came to the house looking for you. You can't run. You can't run from federal officers."

I knew things were very serious, and I knew my mom was right.

"Just come see me," she said.

"I'm too far away," I replied.

But just like a mom, her patience won. "I'll give you a couple of days."

Two days later, I met her for breakfast at Bob Evans.

There is no love comparable to a mother's love, no length of time when it will expire, and no location you can go to escape it.

As I sat at the restaurant table, I could see the devastation on her face. The only other time I had ever seen her this sorrowful and depleted was after my father died. Now I was looking at the same sort of grief, and it was all because of me and my actions. I was her youngest, her baby boy. After me, the doctors told her she couldn't have any more children. I was born on Thanksgiving—which was her birthday too. Each of her tears sliced me like a knife. Watching her grieve the inevitable loss of her son was death by a thousand cuts. She cried and cried. I knew I couldn't run again.

This is it. I'm done.

I thought of my father and how ashamed he would have been. I thought of the opportunities I had been too afraid to take because I felt like a failure after being kicked out of college. I thought again of what a deceased hustler told me once: "There are no 401(k) plans for drug dealers."

Gandhi once said, "All crime is a kind of disease and should be treated as such." It had been my decision and mistake to take a criminal therapeutic; it treated only the symptoms, not the disease. I had to face the consequences of not being able to find relief from an ill society.

I had to turn myself in.

CHAPTER EIGHT

Tragedy Interrupted

It's not failure but aiming too low,
that is life's greatest tragedy.
—Benjamin E. Mays

My adulthood dreams were reduced to wearing a blue jumpsuit and being escorted to an isolated white cell. Nothing feels worse than this. The cold constriction of the handcuffs on your wrists with a chain leading to the cuffs on your feet welcomes you to a unique brotherhood of the disinherited. You know immediately that the outside world is no longer relevant; you are entombed inside the walls, but there is no funeral. That's what prison feels like.

I had tried to avoid this place since childhood, but the criminal justice system had finally received me. I would

136

emerge a number instead of a name. My destiny was going to be written on the steel bars, concrete floors, and cinder blocks.

They called this prison The Cut. The blunt nickname was an apt description. On the outside, the towering red brick fortress resembled the prison from *The Shawshank Redemption;* on the inside, the place was like San Quentin. Built in 1878, the Maryland House of Correction in Jessup was an outdated prison with a history of violence, riots, and escapes. It sat on an embankment, and it received its nickname partially from the nearby railroad tracks that cut through the countryside. The name stuck because of the brutality inside the prison walls. This was a place that left scars.

When I turned myself in, my mom was still living in Columbia, Maryland. I went down to the Howard County Detention Center (HCDC), hoping they would keep me there, as it was a relatively good facility. I was told that they needed to hold me somewhere until they could arraign me, that they had to send me to wherever the federal officers ordered me to go. Instead of my remaining in HCDC, they shipped me off to The Cut. I figured I wouldn't be there for too long. They brought me to a 23/7 cell where I was allowed to come out only for an hour a day to shower, shave, or do whatever I needed to do. It wasn't just solitary confinement; it was a place that concealed hope. The first time the steel door slammed shut, the vibration shook reality into my soul.

This is it. This is unquestionable. Those cinder blocks are going to be my view for the rest of my life. Behind these walls you cannot hide from the truth.

There is nothing like hearing your prison door shutting for the first time. It's a sound I will never forget. The eerie clank of the mechanical door sounds for seconds, and when it's finished making noise, the resulting silence notifies you that you are, for all normal purposes, forgotten.

As I sat in the square, bleak cell with a skinny, long window on the door and another small window high above me, I felt the terror of the possibilities awaiting me. I faced up to thirty years for my charge. I knew I was guilty, but was my potential sentence just?

Justice is a central concept in both morality and law, political philosophy and political practice. We extend justice to individuals and their actions, the rules we set, and the public policies we make. We believe in justice so strongly that if the rules or policies we set are found to be unjust, it is a compelling, if not definitive, justification to oppose them in each case.

Yet the underbelly of criminal justice is ugly. Underneath the surface of this virtue that we hold dear is a monster in the machine. It seems like our culture has a need to produce villains in order to "function." Justice is powerful and important, but the ugly side to it is that it can perpetuate itself and thrive only if it has a villain. We've created a culture of punishment. It's easier to punish people when you dehumanize them. That's how you justify mandatory minimum sentences to assuage public anger. Mandatory minimum sentences are often applied to nonviolent drug offenders. The sentences that individuals receive are governed by the law and only the law, compelling courts to severely prosecute people who pose the least physical threat to the community. Mandatory minimums may have been intended to promote justice, but they have often created a miscarriage of justice in the courtroom, contributing to mass incarceration.

We tell ourselves that justice is blind. Maybe, but justice is not deaf. What I wrestled with in my cell was, Who had the ear of justice? Would I, or would the prosecutor? Prosecutors possess enormous power. They determine which charges to file and whether to request pretrial detention or bail, and they frequently have power over a plea-bargaining procedure. Prosecutors determine how long the defendants remain in prison—and all of this power is supported by the incentives to keep people behind bars.

What are the alternatives to incarceration? We used to have drug courts. What about a problem-solving court? What about community disputes? There are different ways of thinking about this. Prosecutors basically have a blank check to put people in prison. Prosecutors are championed, and they have no incentive other than putting people into the system.

I sat in my cell wondering if the prosecutor would villainize me. Could he or she see me differently? What would it look like if lawyers had an incentive to reduce incarceration and recidivism? I thought about the enormous amount of trauma and failure that had transpired in my life and the weight I carried that, by extension, had led me to this cell.

Every year, the United States releases more than six hundred thousand inmates from federal or state incarceration and cycles more than nine million people through local jails. Recidivism—a person's proclivity to relapse into a previous condition or behavior, especially regression into *criminal* behavior—is normal. Within three years after their release, two out of every three individuals are rearrested, and about half are imprisoned again. According to the Bureau of Prisons, housing *per prisoner* costs between $34,000 and $37,000 a year. Hearing that number may make you think we should create a harsher environment, but the worse the jail conditions and term, the greater the risk of recidivism. Making jail more miserable than it currently is would not save money in the long run; however, it would guarantee that the annual amount is more likely to be spent for the rest of an inmate's life.

I was in pretrial detention, which means I hadn't been convicted of a crime yet. I had to wait for my arraignment, which I was told would happen in a few days, but that wasn't true in my case. I had never been arrested before, so I didn't know what to really expect. I used to hear people talk about the experience of going to jail, but you can't really know until it's you.

They smacked me with a RICO charge. When they first told me that the charges were for fraud, I laughed. "Oh, really? You're arresting me for *fraud*?" I found it hilarious that they didn't seem to care about the drugs. But then my situation began to sink in. I was shocked by the racketeering claim. That part was not so funny. In case you're unfamiliar with it, it's a charge commonly brought by prosecutors against the Mafia or the highly organized and brutal cartels. *I didn't hurt anybody,* I thought. *We couldn't have possibly been* that *organized.* Both of these assumptions were wrong.

Back in my cell, I found myself unable to even pray for God to intervene. I accepted my plight. *This is the place you always knew you would end up,* a hopeless, familiar voice whispered inside me. *This is the place you tried to avoid. But you couldn't. You couldn't. You were always going to end up here.*

It is clear to me now that my education had prepared me to be a prisoner. Childhood surroundings taught me simultaneously that not all life is valued, that no training in trust would be provided, and that safety was absent from my world. Society etched the shady psychology of dehumanization in my mind, licensing me to disassociate from reality. I felt disinherited. Feelings of disgust were easier to appropriate than acts of empathy. The measure of my achievement was not indicative in the adversities I'd overcome but noted in my ability to be stuck in survival mode. I learned to live moment to moment without stopping to think about the future. Like the cinder block walls that engulfed me, scarcity was fixed in my mind.

Prison gives you plenty of time to think—its only positive attribute. It forces you to face yourself, to contemplate why you are there. I found no room for victimhood within those walls, only space to contemplate my decisions. And my thoughts couldn't have been clearer: I didn't want this life.

Since I wasn't a violent offender and since they didn't catch me selling drugs, maybe I would get less of a sentence. The fear of becoming another number lost forever in those walls shrieked like an alarm clock: *Wake up, Michael.* I was afraid.

But maybe I could rebuild my life after this, I reasoned. I had played a risky game and lost. I would be going away for a stretch—I could accept that. *Do your time, then get yourself together, Michael,* I thought.

And I kept staring at those walls, as the light from my little window rose and darkened and rose again for twenty-three hours of every day.

It is not our experiences that make or break us. It's our interpretations of them that ultimately make the difference.

Growing up in church, I was told that God is able, that He can do anything, that nothing is too hard for Him. Most of that rang hollow after my father died. I lacked spiritual "ears to hear," but my natural eye was focused enough to see the self-serving presumptions that Christians often attached to faith. When atrocities occur, claiming God's will is one way to pass the buck, to try to minimize the pain of it. Another way is to blame someone or simply run away from it in outright denial. These are the usual fight-or-flight pathways we take when we don't understand why or how bad things happen to us. Immature religion protects its own privilege.

The comfort of putting our troubles into "good" or "evil" categories or the often-unrealistic black-or-white worldviews (where everyone is simply either a hero or a villain) conceals the power of faith. Or seems to, at least. But at what expense?

Of course, I see now that there is another way to relate to our pain: to be *transformed* by suffering. This, though, requires the acceptance of paradox, and for all its good points, the religion that I had been exposed to when I was young did not think that way.

To pass the time, I tried to work out in the tiny space. But no number of push-ups or jailhouse squats was enough to transform the pain that I carried. I wanted answers, but I felt I'd been asking the wrong questions. In my mind, I could see the words that the preacher used during my father's funeral as if painted on my prison walls: *the Lord takes away.*

My punitive image of God made it easy for me to project my own bitterness and vengeance on Him. I thought He was still taking things away from me. Blaming God was a wordless admission that I had nowhere to place my pain. I ran, I fought, and I even lived in denial to cope with losing my father and my dreams. But it was that very blame that made me open the Bible. It was the only book that was in my cell. And after six weeks in The Cut, I finally began to read it.

O LORD, thou hast searched me, and known me.
Thou knowest my downsitting and mine uprising, thou
understandest my thought afar off. (Psalm 139:1–2)

After six weeks waiting for my arraignment, still nothing had been communicated to me about when the process would move forward. I was ready to plead guilty just to get it over with. Restless and pacing my cell, I wanted to know what was in this book that had caused generations in my family to herald its message.

Thou hast beset me behind and before, and laid thine
hand upon me. (verse 5)

My father and mother had been preachers. Here I was, a prisoner. Mom beseeched God while I berated Him. I wanted nothing to do with Him, yet still somehow I couldn't escape the words I was reading.

Whither shall I go from thy spirit? or whither shall I flee
from thy presence? (verse 7)

Why couldn't He just leave me alone? Pain was my new passport to the world. It was all I had left.

> If I ascend up into heaven, thou art there: if I make my
>   bed in hell, behold, thou art there. (verse 8)

I kept rehearsing my anger, and it had brought me to the closest hell on earth I could find, but I kept reading even when the lights went out. In the darkness God was still searching for me.

> If I say, Surely the darkness shall cover me; even the
>   night shall be light about me.
> Yea, the darkness hideth not from thee; but the night shi-
>   neth as the day: the darkness and the light are both
>   alike to thee. (verses 11–12)

As I kept reading, I wanted to release the habitual aggression that characterized my avoidance of dealing with uncomfortable things. I was wounded, but perhaps my wounds were my way out. I realized that there was no need to hide what God was saying He could handle. Darkness and light are the same to Him. My heart was as hard as the cinder blocks surrounding me. Yet deep down, I wanted to believe that I was on God's mind and that He was on my side. Belief can limit you or launch you. I was tired of building up evidence that dissuaded me from God's love. I was open to letting go of every suspicion I held about the goodness of God.

> How precious also are thy thoughts unto me, O God!
>   how great is the sum of them!
> If I should count them, they are more in number than
>   the sand: when I awake, I am still with thee.
>   (verses 17–18)

One Sunday morning in my cell, the steel door rumbled open and a guard told me to get up. "Your lawyer's waiting," the guard told me.

I was confused. Nothing happens on a Sunday, so I had no idea why I was being taken anywhere, especially with my lawyer. They escorted me out of the Maryland House of Correction and put me in a van. I was led into a judge's chambers where my lawyer sat looking through a stack of papers. He motioned me to a chair next to him. As I sat down, I could feel my whole body shaking. A lawyer from the prosecutor's office was there, but the judge hadn't arrived yet. I surveyed the room, noticing different things like the fact that there was no nameplate on the judge's desk. Hanging on the wall behind the desk was a framed poster of Leonardo da Vinci's famous drawing *The Vitruvian Man.* I stared at the male figure standing with his arms and legs apart in both a circle and a square and thought we both had something in common.

Though in different ways, we both had been stripped bare, ready to be made over.

The judge walked into the office. He wore a pair of slacks held up by suspenders and a button-down shirt. He found his robe and slipped it on right in front of us, then sat down without introducing himself. The judge picked up some of the papers and leafed through them for a few moments before he began to talk.

"I am scheduled to arraign you on Monday," he began, "where you will officially enter into a plea. However . . ." He paused. "Your attorney has told me you were accepted to multiple colleges and that you recently lost your scholarship due to a car accident. Is that true?"

"Yes, sir." There was so much pain behind that acknowledgment of reality. *Where is he going with this?* I wondered.

"Michael, the prosecutor, your attorney, and I have discussed this, and we've all agreed. There is a program called Give Me a Chance we want to place you in. It is designed to provide adjudicated youth the opportunity to go to college instead of prison." My head was spinning even before he got to his question. "Do you want to go to jail, or do you want to go to college?"

I'm not sure if my words even came out right because my response was so quick: "I want to go to college."

The judge with no name did not go into a lengthy monologue about what I had done or the opportunity that was being given. He did not berate or belittle me. Instead, he encouraged me. He told me, in very few words, that this was the shot of a lifetime; don't throw it away.

"You have a purpose," the judge told me. "Use this opportunity to rebuild your life with help from God and others. Today I represent the first deposit that others will give; the rest is up to you and God."

He stood up, took off his robe, and walked out of the room. The charges against me were dropped. My case was sealed. Today, the only sign that I ever had a brush with the criminal justice system is the traffic ticket I received for driving without a license. I would never have to "check the box" on an application for employment.

I was nearly nineteen years old and ready for a second chance. The hand of Providence had blotted out my transgressions.

What moved the judge's heart to snatch me from the fire could be equated only to the Lord's doing. I found out later that the prosecutor had become convinced that I was a pawn in the dangerous game I had been playing and not a king. My attorney had gone to my house and pulled a letter out of the box of college acceptance and scholarship offers without my knowledge. The letter happened to be from Oral Roberts University. Prior to my arrest, a gentleman named Bill Owens had come to my mother's church from ORU to talk about the Give Me a Chance program. I remember him standing up in front of the congregation, looking directly at me, and saying, "There is no doubt in my heart that Michael Phillips will significantly impact the world." I remember thinking at that moment that Bill was crazy and had no clue what he was talking about.

How does one judge potential? Bill could see I had something. So could the judge, but being in the wrong lane for too long had obscured my view. Yet success was still available, even though it was hidden within me. The same day, I was sent home to pack my bags and leave for Oral Roberts University. It was surreal; I felt like I had been dead, and yet there I was back in my own room—a door I could open, a window I could see out of—*alive.*

I was ready to find out what was next. I was ready for redemption.

Transformation starts when something old is allowed to fall apart, not when a new experience begins. I was just shy of nineteen years old and facing thirty years in prison. If I had gotten the full charge, I might still be in jail for a year of foolishness. I cannot tell you the level of gratitude I have toward Bill Owens; he was on a mission to save as many as he could. The Give Me a Chance program was an incredible opportunity. And I cannot tell you the amount of thanks I have for the judge, whose name I have never been able to learn, and the prosecutor, whom I never met. They changed my life forever.

Packing my clothes for my new adventure filled me with both appreciation and panic. While grateful for a second chance, the fear of starting over again overshadowed my excitement at the opportunity. What would be my story? A more frightening question was, Would society relate to my experience? When avoiding pain is higher in value than creating our dreams, our actions dictate we avoid the emotional exposure. I needed to love myself and the vision for my life enough to see if it could truly exist. I had to let the emotional chips fall where they may. It was the only way I was going to be able to get on that plane.

The good news is that faith operates in the atmosphere of uncertainty. I wasn't sure how things were going to turn out, but I decided while flying over the country toward ORU that the luggage I brought with me was not nearly as important as the baggage I needed to leave behind. Reflecting on the unexpected emotional turmoil led me to also think about how many friends I'd lost and how many young men who look like me were still behind bars and how many young men who look like me were still left behind.

When children are left behind, they become adults who are left behind. We used to see beautiful billboards throughout our community with images of individuals who looked like us smoking cigarettes or drinking their favorite dark liquor. But I never saw a billboard with a hedge fund manager that looked like me. I never saw a scientist or engineer up there. The irony of telling us we have control over our lives while placing us under the constant influence of negative images would be rich if it wasn't so destructive. I wish when I was a kid there was a billboard that showed me the amount of money I could make over my life span if I got a high school diploma or a college degree versus the amount of money I would get paid as an inmate. If my neighborhood had billboards that exposed us to more and informed us of the world of possibilities, then perhaps there would not be so many of us behind bars, left behind, or dead.

We grow up afraid of the police and people in our own neighborhoods, aware that we don't even need to commit a crime to be arrested or killed. We are constantly disappointed by the very people who are charged to protect us. When others' low expectations for you assume your fate to be prison or worse, it doesn't leave you with a healthy optimism for community or your own chances. To make matters worse, society notices our rage but not our pain, so we retain the trauma and make it ours.

"Trauma decontextualized . . . in a people looks like culture."

Thirty thousand feet in the air and I felt like my feet were still on the ground. To a traumatized individual, there is only now. Most of the horrible things that happened in my life never got acknowledged. They continued to build inside me, fusing themselves to my nervous system. It impacted everything: how I thought, how I behaved, and how I reacted to stress. Seeing someone murdered at ten years of age. Having to fight every day just to go to school. Losing my father. Breaking my leg and losing my scholarship. Going to prison.

As horrible as those things were, I tried to imagine myself healed. I wanted to start the healing process before I landed in Tulsa.

The things I did were not who I was.

Most people confuse what they did with who they are. Because they did those things, they start believing they *are* those things, telling themselves they're failures. But they're not failures. You might have failed, but you're not a failure. Part of the recipe for mediocrity is to become your own judge. Flaws don't make us failures; they make us unique. I fought off the guilt and shame on that flight because guilt shrinks destiny. I wasn't going back behind bars, back to the solitary cell in The Cut. I was out and free and facing my future.

CHAPTER NINE

Redemption and Reentry

Only society make rules where my people suffer and that
[is] why we must have redemption and redemption now.

—BOB MARLEY

After 1,229 miles, we prepared for arrival. When the wheels came down on the runway, the sound of the screeching brakes was music to my ears. I had landed on the other side of tragedy. When I deboarded the plane, like most people in a new place, I looked for the signs that would tell me which way to go. The distance from the gate to baggage claim stretched indefinitely; I stumbled forward, really searching for the signpost that would become my instructions, telling me how to start over. Moving onward can be only a conscious choice; I wish it were as easy as reading "Baggage claim this way," but forward progress often comes with barriers. Especially for people who have a lot of baggage.

State and federal criminal history archives include more than 110 million criminal history records. These files are the baggage of millions of Americans who suffer substantial obstacles in their attempts to reintegrate into society and are usually denied the chance to shed the shadow of their criminal histories. They contend with not only social shame but also more than forty thousand legal "collateral consequences" that impair their ability to become entrepreneurs, acquire work, vote, locate a decent place to reside, and become positive contributors in their local communities.

Collateral consequences are spread across state and federal legislative and regulatory codes and are often unnoticed by those charged with their management and implementation. There is a lack of coordination between various portions of state and federal regulations, which makes it difficult to determine all the penalties and limitations associated with a specific conviction. Additionally, the repercussions apply to the individuals attempting to reenter society regardless of the amount of time that has passed between their convictions and the rehabilitation efforts following their convictions.

Redemption will always require reentry.

Almost everyone who is jailed is ultimately released back into our communities. More than ten thousand individuals are released each week from state and federal prisons. We say that once people leave prison, they have paid their debts to society, but in actuality we burden them by placing their criminality in the luggage that they carry for a lifetime. If previously incarcerated individuals are to overcome the internal and external barriers, they will need what Dr. Carrie Pettus-Davis calls the 5-Key Model: meaningful work trajectories, effective coping strategies, positive social engagement, positive relationships, and healthy thinking patterns. When combined, these five keys can increase the overall well-being of previously incarcerated individuals and decrease the likelihood of their returning to criminal behavior.

Second chances can turn into third, fourth, fifth, and sixth chances. Sometimes we demand that people with a past walk around with catcher's mitts on both hands, taking every ball thrown at them and never throwing any back. We bemoan their requests for dignity, and resolve that they are nothing more than the crimes they committed. Out of frustration some of them decide to throw something back.

I wondered while waiting at baggage claim how much suspicion I would have to take, but right at the moment I started to feel alone, Bill Owens showed up. Thank God that some people still believe in second chances.

Waiting for my bags at the airport, I recalled some of my childhood dreams. They were never truly lost. Like the luggage that tumbles down the conveyor belt, it is just a matter of time before we pick up what's ours. Standing there in a new city with a new chance, I decided I wouldn't let what was professedly lost go unclaimed.

It is okay to begin with nothing. It is okay to start over. You just have to start. Getting in the white van with the other nine students in the Give Me a Chance program, I found it hard to know whether I would be welcomed, but the flat landscape of Oklahoma rolled out like a red carpet. Even the stoplights of Tulsa seemed filled with grace—we hit only the greens on our twenty-minute ride to campus. Turning onto Lewis Avenue, I couldn't help but feel a sense of gratitude. But the all-too-familiar grief was present also. I was entering a new world.

When I saw the towering statue of two praying hands sitting at the edge of the golden City of Faith, the unyielding negative evaluation within handcuffed me to history, my destiny undistinguishably chained to yesterday. I knew when I stepped out of the van I would struggle to begin again. The driver told us about the praying hands (modeled after Oral Roberts' and his son's hands) cast from thirty tons of bronze. Inscribed in the middle of the figure are the words *Educating the whole man.*

I stared at those words, trying to shake a feeling of unworthiness.

How could I measure up to this place? The entire campus was like entering an alternate dimension, its buildings designed with a striking midcentury retro-future architecture. Every building seemed to point upward, their very walls saying *hope.* I was fascinated—all of this came out of the vision of one man.

I hoped I could live up to my second chance. I was already concerned I would lack the power to adapt and would turn to negative "solutions" to ease the strain.

Bill Owens greeted us at the athletic center where registration was taking place. We came from across the country, all of us with shared similar troubled backgrounds. We walked inside as he shared some of the rules. There was a requirement to attend church on Sundays; you had to be out of your dorm room by ten o'clock in the morning. He also highlighted the student ID as being extremely important. It was your permit to get food, register for classes, and even get into the dorms. To get a student ID, men had to shave—as in no hair on your face. Asking a Black man to get rid of his goatee felt like telling Superman to lose his cape.

I flipped out. "*No.* I will not shave." Bill had to take me into the bathroom to remind me of this truth: if I wasn't going to change my mind, then what difference would a new location make? It sunk in that I was about to dismiss a new experience at the expense of my growth. If I decided to forgo this opportunity over a trivial matter, who was to say that I would get another chance? I had never shaved with a straight razor before, but I chose to heed his advice, and I reluctantly hacked the hair off my chin.

Suddenly baby-faced, I realized how unprepared I was for this place. There were not too many people who looked like me. Even after I found my people, the feeling of being a fish out of water was exaggerated when I got a better look at the fishbowl. The student lounge where all the Black people mostly gathered was surrounded by glass, placed in the newest dorm building. I had never belonged to anything that looked or felt this pure. The university being predominately White (both in student body and faculty) didn't bother me as much as it being predominately *wholesome*. The school was everything I was not. There was no one on the campus that I wanted to mentor me, but more hazardous to my development was that there was no one I wanted to model.

I couldn't relate to the rules, the campus, or the culture, but I wanted to make the best of it. Admittedly there was a nondescript specialness to the school, and part of that secret sauce was the students. The majority of them had a radical optimism that was curiously contagious. They really *believed* in something. I made friends very quickly, but because of their authentic zeal, I kept them at arm's length. I simply couldn't fully understand it. And I think I was afraid that my own internal darkness would be contagious somehow, that like a yawn passed from person to person, my trauma would spread to others. They all spoke so openly. I didn't want to go there. I didn't want to talk about my past, and I thought it was safer not to have many people around me. Gradually I pulled back from the friendships that had begun.

Choosing to live anonymously to deal with adversity was a bad habit that I formed. I had been delivered from jail, but

I was still not free. Deliverance is not freedom; deliverance is preparation for freedom. Without the necessary will to do the required work of change, I returned to my default setting.

In my mind, college was supposed to be about developing the whole person, like the statue had suggested—an environment where I could cultivate my potential and build skills. But in my stress and confusion, I chose to work on my vices rather than my virtues. The easiest path is the one you believe is most possible, so I took the road I knew best, a road that led me back to what I had learned to do: profit from pain, both mine and other people's.

I started little businesses on the side, providing weed to interested people in the area and selling TVs and clothes to some of the students. It wasn't much, just a little to make some money. My only supervision was my being in school.

I was smoking a lot more weed and drinking more often than I ever had, and I refused to go to church on Sundays. I even warned my resident advisor one day, telling him if he knocked on my door again on a Sunday morning to go to church, I was gonna knock him out. The next week he had me reassigned to another floor.

I quickly became the bad boy in Tulsa and earned the moniker Demon-seed on campus. I was a pariah, and students began to get hints from the faculty and staff to stay away from me.

I found a safe harbor in North Tulsa. My roommate's sister lived in an apartment complex that gave me familiar surroundings and the cover to operate yet another side business: selling weed and cigarettes. But it didn't last long. One night close to midnight, I decided to stay over instead of returning to campus for class. My roommate's sister sat next to me and looked me in the eyes.

"What are you doing here?" she asked me.

"I thought you knew I was spending the night."

"That's not what I mean."

The words she spoke next felt like a wrecking ball. "You don't belong here. This is not who you are. It would be a shame if you continued on this path only to die before you discover who you are." My facade splintered under the weight of those words.

I lay there that night, wrestling with what she had said. I knew she was right. I had hardly even begun on my second chance, and already I was throwing it away. This path had one end.

Why should I die and make the graveyard rich?

I had reached the tipping point. The door to my heart had been cracked open, and something different had been let in. Returning to campus with clarity gave me the momentum to let go and move forward. ORU might not have been my preference, but I believed and knew with certainty it was where I needed to be. Trying to belong there became less important than working on myself. I embraced the college experience because I could no longer live in the bounds of what I tolerated.

Collegiate environments don't teach us who we are, but they provide the platforms to discover new pathways. I learned that when we bemoan the inability to discover our purpose, we are really lamenting the lack of having a clear path. So, every incident, accident, and mistake lifts us up into the dark clouds of our deepest fears. Those fears convince us that who we long to be remains nebulous and what we long to accomplish remains untouchable. But having someone believe in your potential (like my judge) or someone who calls you out and expects more from you (like my roommate's sister) is like air sinking into a cloud. It's grace. Grace dissipated my fogginess, and mercy gave my feet gravity.

Attending services at the spring revival at Oral Roberts University was mandatory. I couldn't threaten my RA and tell him I wasn't going to go. If I didn't attend, then I wouldn't get my credits for that semester. I had to go. Although I was ready to straighten up, I still didn't want to be in anyone's sanctuary. If I had to go, then I was going to do it my way. I decided to get as high as I could possibly get. I wanted to be as numb as I could. So before the revival service, I rolled and smoked five blunts and drank a fifth of vodka and a few beers.

I didn't feel a thing after that. I was numb enough to go to church. In a chapel that sat thousands of people, they put me and my friends in the third row. *Why they got me in the third row?* I wondered. We were all high and laughing, clapping and mocking those around us. Spring revival brought out a whole bunch of big-name preachers and famous singers onto the stage. While I was in my seat, the singers got up and began to sing "How Great Thou Art."

O Lord my God, when I in awesome wonder
Consider all the worlds Thy hands have made
I see the stars, I hear the rolling thunder
Thy power throughout the universe displayed.

Then sings my soul, my Savior God, to Thee
How great Thou art, how great Thou art
Then sings my soul, my Savior God, to Thee
How great Thou art, how great Thou art!

All of a sudden, I began to cry, and before I knew it, I was sober. I started to feel what my grandmother used to sing about: "Blessed Assurance." I felt peace and I felt love. It terrified me. My former way of carrying my burdens was being challenged, and I was too accustomed to the weight that it became too unpleasant to lay it down. Vulnerable and open, I jumped out of my seat and ran up the middle aisle, trying to get away. All of my friends saw me crying and running out of the room.

The momentary brush with grace did not feel graced. It felt like the old me was dying. I was exhausted and trying to escape God's presence. Trying to escape my own freedom. Trying to keep the pain that had become my comfort zone. One hundred yards back to my dorm room, I stormed in and slammed the door.

"Leave me alone," I uttered out loud. "Just leave me alone."

The walls of another isolated room surrounded me. The same room I ran back to after seeing Raymond shot dead on a corner in front of me. The same space where I railed at God after losing my father. The same confinement I found myself in after the car crash. The same solitary cell that I spent six weeks in. The same cell I made for myself time and time again because I unleashed my anger but buried my ache.

God had followed me, and I couldn't get away. I reached out to the one person whom I knew could help me, who could give me some advice or at least could calm me. Calling my mom, I began to speak to her but couldn't really get any words out. I mumbled incoherent words through my tears, telling her what happened.

"Oh, baby," my mother said in a calm and assured tone. "God's just dealing with you."

Then she hung up, and I was left alone with my maker.

I got down on my knees. "Okay, God. What do You want from me?"

For the next thirty minutes, I sat in the presence of God for the first time, and I knew it was Him. Vacant but receptive, like a blank page waiting for new words, I humbly waited. An overwhelming sense of calm and peace came over me. The anger and frustrations were gone.

There's something in this room with me that's immense.

For the first time in a very long time, I felt safe. This intangible thing in the room with me began to give me very tangible and crystal-clear whispers on what my life looked like and what I was meant to do. I wasn't unconscious or hovering out of my body. I kneeled and I knew what He was telling me.

You are called to preach, Michael. You are called to inspire. This is who you are. This is the purpose for your life.

The same purpose I began to dream about before my father passed away.

When I heard a knocking on my door, I opened it and saw my RA.

"You good?" he asked me. He looked alarmed, as if he were seeing something strange.

"Yeah, I'm okay. Why you got a crazy look on your face?" I asked.

"We thought you, like, overdosed or something in there."

I laughed. "What are you talking about? Why would you say something like that?"

"Mike—you've been in there for three days, dude."

"What?"

"Yeah, it's been three days," my RA said.

It had felt like thirty minutes to me. God had me in His presence for three whole days, doing surgery on my mind, doing surgery on my heart and on my spirit.

"Man, you look completely different," he told me.

"I feel like I need to tell everybody what happened," I said. My RA gathered some of the guys on the floor, and I shared my testimony.

To be made well, kept safe, and preserved is what it means to be saved. It is the essence of atonement or (as I think of it) at-one-ment. I never really understood why the cross was chosen as the symbol of the Christian faith until God's peace followed me into my room. The cross is the collision of opposites. Jesus hung between two thieves, holding the mystery of suffering without demanding the perfection or acceptance of either thief. He died for both, but only one would come into relationship with Christ while he was on the cross. All of my angst toward God came from the fallacy that I believed as a hurt child: I believed that God only takes away. But I realized that it was pain that had been my thief.

Relationship is the key to understanding religion, because God is found in all things—in the trauma, the tragedy, the sinful, and, yes, in the pain. Human and divine, on the cross Jesus was visibly broken yet entirely whole. The cross is simultaneously the worst and best moment in history. That's exactly where I was: broken but longing to be made whole, imperfect but entirely accepted. Old things had finally passed away, and all things had become new.

When you don't understand the dark seasons of your life, it's natural to want to escape or to fight in anger. But the darkness isn't real; it is the consequence of light leaving your life. These are some of the most painful times we can experience. But inside the weary agony and the intruding numbness, we still might discover the depths of our strength and our courage and transition to a new life. Don't run from it. Without the backdrop of darkness, there would be no contrast; there would be nothing to see. Darkness doesn't have to disappear for the light to shine inside it. Conversely, we must also know that the light is always present even in our darkest moments. It's why we dream. When the night is all around us, we dream.

Your dream is your map.

The route that you take to get there prepares you for the destination, but the destination can never prepare you for the route.

There are chasms you're going to have to cross.

There are gaps you're going to have to navigate.

There are detours on that map that want to devour you. There are delays. There might even be a detention center or prison on that map, but none of those things should deter you from going after your dreams. My life was full of twists and turns and inconvenient paradoxes, but as the old saints would say, "Troubles don't last always." God wasn't through with me, and He's not through with you.

It's not too late. It's never too late as long as you have breath in your body.

CHAPTER TEN

No Success
Without Struggle

What and how much had I lost trying to do
only what was expected of me instead of what
I myself had wished to do?
—RALPH ELLISON in *Invisible Man*

The painful parts of my story could have been told a million times by a million people. The fundamental question we must ask ourselves is *why?* While we hold dear the argument of societal improvement, it seems that those efforts constantly result in unimproved societal conclusions. "The more things stay the same, the less things change." Our collective ailments stem from the pain in our communal brains. We suffer from the same story. Struggle is common. Pain is pervasive. But these are the old anecdotes that we have given mental and cultural real estate to, leaving little room to imagine a better way. The zero-sum framework that we put around our society fosters despair, making it more difficult for some to color in a brighter future.

Our belief systems, culture, and values exist by choice.

It's not a question of if we have the power to upgrade them but rather if we (as a society) have the will.

When we collectively cede the power to shape what could be to what has always existed, we become increasingly cynical and overwhelmingly divisive. Like white ink on a white page, we don't show up for one another anymore. We have decided who deserves help and who does not; then we institutionalized that idea. How good are our policies if they don't bring people to a sense of purpose and possibility? Our social constructs have produced in the present only what already existed in the past. This is not a criticism of intent but rather an observation of the reality that we have created. The fallout of our good ideological pursuits punishes people severely for small mistakes and penalizes them for having inequitable characteristics, such as the colors of their skins or the zip codes where they live—even down to the granular level of personal troubles, such as divorce, unemployment, illness, or crime. We've turned traumatized experiences into profitable items that our social systems capitalize on.

As it turns out, misery is more marketable than the miraculous.

We each have the power to change that, but do we have the *will*? And if we are concerned about it requiring a miracle to do so, let us remember that a miracle is only a process that has been accelerated. It's not too late to change our societal frame to one that is bound together by a deepened community, committed to creating a culture of possibility, and built on the canvas of purpose inclusive of every color and creed. We are not out of time; we are not out of options.

But to fortify lasting change, we have to listen better and tell a different story. Stories are designed to either move us forward or hold us back. The stories we tell ourselves—and, more importantly, the narratives we choose to believe— matter. What is our societal story? Our systems of education, justice, health, economics, and government have become the hotbed for ostracized people. If we continue to bury that lede, more generations will fall behind.

The very institutions that were designed to offer aid to people instead systematically detect, sort, and repress certain populations while simultaneously gaslighting their stories of hardships and touting the flawed concepts of rugged individualism and the American dream. All of these require assistance from someone at some point along the journey. These outdated orthodoxies do not embolden purpose; they engender chronic social rejection. They lack power because they indirectly negate the sense of possibility, causing all of us to attach ourselves to the weak societal structure of comfortable misery that defends the perception of permanence.

The only way the old guard can prevail is if we fall into the trap of invisibility.

I fell into that snare.

I almost lost everything because I believed what others expected of me.

I had multiple barriers to overcome and significant gaps to leap over. I would have been defeated if it were not for a judge who decided to color outside the lines, a mother who would not stop praying, and an advocate on a mission to save as many as he could. I came extremely close to suffering the penalty of a culture of punishment. Mercy found me. That was the only reason I was not consumed. Under the tutelage of such grace, I had uninhibited access to pursue what I was meant to be. Education became freedom, and purpose became power. When the two met in my life, something cosmic took place. These are the dual forces we must build on for the benefit of the societal whole.

As we noted in chapter 1, the etymology of *educate* indicates that it means to "lead forth" or to "bring out" what is within. Education teaches us the *what* of ourselves, but it cannot tell us the *why* because knowledge is not synonymous with reason. I needed to know that I had purpose, that I mattered. The etymology of *purpose* shows that it means "aim, intention." Purpose gives us the *why,* the target where we can aim our gifts and talents.

If education is the frame, then purpose is the adaptable canvas that stretches over it.

When I went through the difficulty of not knowing why I even existed and questioning my own value, neither instance could eliminate my reason for being. Ignorance of purpose does not nullify purpose, and a lack of education does not cancel the opportunity for education. Both remain available no matter how insignificant one might feel.

As it was for me, so it is for others and for our society at large. How can we give more people access to a sense of purpose and a high-quality education?

Everybody has a story, and everybody is part of a collective story, but what about *the* story? The story is the history of our country. The history of the police force. The history of oppression. It's everything embedded into the fabric of our culture. Until we can be honest about that, we'll never create systems and institutions that fully empower people to live out their purpose. Everything we've built and everything we have in society has been determined by individuals. We need to stop defending the boundary of our collective story. We need to come outside the boundaries of our own circles to listen and learn and understand others.

Solidarity is the greatest form of social justice. If we can at least stand in solidarity, then perhaps we can start to see the systemic changes we want. Another way to look at it is that we have to stop mistaking unity for uniformity. Solidarity is an agreement that you feel me and understand me, but it doesn't mean we have to be uniform. I can stand with you as a human being to understand the inequities without looking like you and dressing like you. Standing with you is simply a start.

We all know that in this world we will have trouble. We all understand that there is no success without struggle, but we err when we conflate hard times with hopeless marginalization. Yes, pain is a part of life, but it's not okay for people to be stigmatized for displacement. Sucking it up cannot be the answer for every circumstance. There are countless people whose stories have gone unheard or who were met with disrespect when listened to. Have we mined those stories to make sense of educational inequities, income inequality, or social justice disparities? Can we even hear those stories without concluding that something is out of place in our society? All the children are *not* well.

How many right turns are waiting to be made?

Culture can be created only collectively. It's something we have to do together. And as we do so, for better or worse, the investments we make in our structures and institutions matter. We have to ask ourselves, Are we choosing to support what we want to see in our communities? When we have more investment in criminal justice than we do in education, we have to question our values. Like the Maasai greeting, our financial support reveals our values. In our country, state and municipal investment in juvenile correction facilities and prisons has exceeded the amount of their expenditures for preschool through twelfth-grade education over the past three decades. From 1989 to 2013, we spent six times more on jails than on higher education.

The things that are right in front of us are often the hardest to see.

On average the total cost per inmate is $33,274, and on average federal, state, and local governments spend $14,840 to educate a child. We know that incarceration is more expensive than education. Yet in some states, we build more prisons than we do schools. If our budgets reflect our belief systems, then it is evident that we have lost hope in human potential and have divested from individual purpose. Our shared selective attention in our culture makes data like this possible. The problems that make the headlines become the foreground while the five-hundred-pound gorilla—our crisis of education, along with the crisis in policing and crisis in economy—walks through the background unnoticed.

That proverbial gorilla represents misinformation (and the information that we miss) about the root causes of our education crisis and hints toward the solution that we need. Regardless of what individual problem has our attention, be it educational disparities, poverty, discrimination, racism, social justice, etc., the fact that the gorilla is in the room with all of us cannot continue to be ignored. At some point, we have to turn to each other and ask, "Hey, did you see that?" and believe each other when we do so. This is the only way to get beneath the symptoms to treat the cause of our problems.

"Culture is the characteristics and knowledge of a particular group of people, encompassing language, religion, cuisine, social habits, music and arts." Culture includes our "patterns of behaviors and interactions, cognitive constructs, and affective understanding that are learned through . . . socialization." But the incredible thing about culture is that, through story, it holds within itself the ability to help and heal those who belong to it. Culture can lift the spirit and link us to our past and to the possibility of our future. It inspires the imagination and galvanizes empathy. And those, together, support individual and collective resilience. If we can extract the power that is within our stories, then we can inspire, teach, clarify, change hearts, and bring healing perspective, ultimately mending generations.

The greatest story individuals can hear is that they have purpose.

My purpose ignited that first Sunday that I gave my testimony. The very next week, I ended up sharing my story at a church in Tampa, Florida. Opening up and telling others about losing my father, about the accident, about losing myself, and about God finding me were exhilarating. The response was even more so. I stood on the platform with no title; they didn't call me pastor, minister, or preacher. The bishop at the church simply said, "A young man would like to share his story." That's when I realized that purpose is more about *being* than about doing.

I was a young man with a story, and telling it became a source of fulfillment to me and encouragement to those who heard it. To be yourself and to express yourself fully define purpose. To keep searching for your innate talents and abilities underscores potential. But sometimes we need to hear or see purpose and potential in someone we identify with in order for us to discover our own. After I shared my story, I looked up and saw the altar full of young men and women who were in search of the same thing. I was not alone in my experience, and neither were they.

Later that month, a man named Joseph Jennings invited me to a big youth rally in Los Angeles, with thousands of gang members attending. Jennings was a former gang member who worked with youth, deterring them from the dangers of drug use, gang violence, and other risky behaviors.

This was the first time I ever opened the Bible and preached from a text. It was Isaiah 46:10, "Declaring the end from the beginning and from ancient times things not yet done, saying, 'My purpose shall stand, and I will fulfill my intention'" (NRSV). There was that word: *purpose.* It lifted off the page like a 747 taking us thirty thousand feet in the air. It didn't matter that I didn't know how to preach; I stood there knowing why I needed to preach. I could see myself in the different shapes and colors in the audience. I could see the individuals' value. I told my story, and I reminded them of theirs. I told them there was something already finished that they were born to start because God never begins with the beginning; He starts with the end in mind. He starts with purpose. I continued, saying, "God made you from a unique mold, then threw it away after you were completed. Your existence is evidence that this generation needs something that your life contains. Your purpose is necessary, and there is no substitute for you. Your childhood dreams were your destiny screaming at you. Pick those dreams back up. Don't judge your destiny by where you were born or whom you were born to. You're not a mistake, and you're not *going to be* a winner, because you already are."

Every time I said the word *purpose,* it sliced the atmosphere like the Concorde. Looks of relief, gratitude, and newfound joy spread throughout the crowd.

The next day had a greater impact for me than preaching on that massive platform the day before. We got to visit where a few gang members lived. I thought I knew what difficulty was, but I had no clue. Walking a mile in someone else's shoes lets you know immediately that you don't wear the same size. We gathered in an abandoned garage that had been converted into their home. Over thirty people, mostly runaways trying to escape abusive situations, lived in a space that was smaller than the average convenience store with no heat or air conditioning. Dirty mattresses lined the floors. There was only one bathroom. The youngest of the crew was Carlos, only thirteen years old and already tatted up like an OG.

I spent the day listening to their stories, and what stood out the most was the narrative they all shared. Accounts of abandonment and abuse came one after the other, but somehow, though not ideal in many people's eyes, they built their own community out of it. Before I left, Carlos talked with me about the life he wanted. We sat next to a dingy window covered by bars as I listened to him intently. He wanted to explore the stars. He wanted to be an astronaut.

Sadly his life was taken not long after we spoke.

That was over twenty years ago. But the story today is little different.

Abandonment and abuse—though perhaps not exactly like the gang members experienced—are what we have collectively inflicted. We have vacated certain social problems that we have the power to take on. If we chose to invest in purpose rather than punishment, abuse would not be inevitable. We could decide as a society that all children are valuable, and the conventional wisdom to invest in them early on would pay off handsomely in terms of their productivity and development, as well as the unspeakable benefits it would bring to us overall. But instead of saving society a great deal of money and pain, we choose to institutionalize our social problems. That way the social pain we've experienced, which is part of all of us, now becomes viewed as individualistic. And each story of marginalization can be dismissed very easily with an individual's narrative of pulling herself up by her bootstraps. But when your boots have been taken or never provided, it becomes impossible to pull on what doesn't exist.

The gang members I visited exhibited all the things that we've come to hold dear in our culture: grit, determination, and even character—so much so that they were willing to risk their lives for the hope of life, liberty, and happiness. Yet they were still at the bottom of society. They were still marginalized. Of course there is no excuse for crime, and I am not trying to excuse the violence and destruction that come with such a life. But when our youth turn their vast potential into lives of crime or vice, they are the symptom of a sick culture, not the disease.

Individual purpose, not individual pain, has to become entrenched in the framework of our culture and policies if we are going to change our societal story. Two decades after speaking with Carlos, I stood in another room with a young man, having a conversation near an eerily similar murky window covered by bars on the outside—but this time it was in a classroom.

He was a third grader standing in the corner of his science class. *There's no way that we are still making kids stand in*

the corner for disciplinary reasons in the twenty-first century,
I thought to myself. I walked over, got down on one knee, and
tapped him on the shoulder. I said, "How you doing? My
name is Michael Phillips." The response I got from the young
man was not the one I thought I would get because I had been
told that he always stood in the corner and that he had be-
havioral issues.

This young man turned around, bright eyed with confidence, shook my hand, and said, "Hi, my name is Calvin."

"Hey, Calvin, are you enjoying your class today?"

"Yes. This is my favorite class."

"Oh man, that's awesome. Calvin, let me ask you a question. Why are you standing up in the corner?"

Calvin looked at me with those bright and brilliant eyes
and said, "Because my chair is broken." He then pointed to
the chair and said, "Every time I sit in that chair, I fall, and
when I fall, I get into trouble. So I'd rather just stand in the
corner and do my work."

For whatever reason, I got down on the floor, and I started
to try to fix his chair. The chair was dated and worn, much
like the rest of the furniture in the disheveled classroom. The
four legs on the chair weren't stable. Investigating, I saw that
the frame of the chair was bent and one of its adjustable legs
was stuck. No wonder he was falling out of it. It wasn't a
perfect job, but I was able to adjust it enough so it was steady
and sat a little bit higher.

I looked at Calvin and said, "Hey, I fixed your chair." Calvin sat in that seat, gave me a big smile, and stuck his chest out like he was ready to soar.

I left the classroom not thinking much of that moment, but when I got halfway down the hall, Calvin came running. Screaming my name, "Mr. Phillips! Mr. Phillips!" he leaped into my arms like he was my child.

"Thank you for fixing my chair," Calvin said. "Now can you help me fix my school?"

I said, "I'm gonna get to work on it."

He ran back to class, and I walked out of that school building trying to figure out how I could help him fix his school because, like Calvin, when our children are forced to learn in broken chairs, they are forced to stand in the corners of our society.

We are constantly told from grade school that we will all have opportunities. That we can become anything, especially if we work hard. Calvin was working hard in a culture of inequality that was mislabeling him as disabled because of a broken chair. He had been suspended several times for standing in the corner. There was nothing cognitively wrong with him or behaviorally problematic. There was simply no one in his personal sphere who was aware of the comical barrier he faced daily in a broken chair. Carlos worked hard to survive the abandonment of his biological parents and the abuse of his foster parents, but the gang he joined couldn't countervail the streets that claimed him.

The social positions of Calvin and Carlos exposed them to structural conditions that made it very easy for them to be locked into a cruel place. And before we second-guess this notion by telling ourselves that we have programs that should have helped them, we must realize that most of those programs are preconceived for the culture, meaning the program fits the culture but often does not fit the person. It's not just the efficacy of our solutions we have to consider; it's also the fit. "One size fits all" doesn't apply.

We cannot separate position from opportunity. When we do, we fail to see the people at the margins. That's where I was brought up—wrestling with how society saw me and how I saw myself, trying to fit into spaces and places that were not purposed for me, and living beneath my potential. My story didn't end there; it was interrupted. An interruption is culturally viewed as a negative thing, but is it really? An interruption is "a stoppage or hindering of an activity for a time." And that's what we all need: a moment to realize that the way we are going is the wrong direction.

A moment to discover a better way. A moment to know that the trouble we face today is not the end.

I wrote this book from hindsight with the hopes that someone might gain insight. With the hope that we would all step into our purposes so that we might interrupt tragedy for another person. I had that hope of purpose early in my life, and I invite you to travel there with me.

When I was ten years old, I jumped off the second-floor balcony of our duplex. You could not convince me that I was not Superman. I leaped! In my Fruit of the Loom Underoos, red Superman boots, and the cape I had gotten for Christmas. Why did I jump? I had an intuitive feeling, this inherent belief (plus I was a little bit crazy). I sensed that I was made for a special mission and built with the power to pull it off. Needless to say, the laws of gravity put my flying skills to the test. The garage roof directly beneath our balcony broke my fall, the clothesline in our yard tangled my legs, and I didn't hit the ground.

I had a few scrapes and bruises, but no bones were broken. My grandmother ran out of the house and found me entangled, crying, and hanging upside down. She unhooked my legs and took me in the house. My sister looked at me with a face that said it all: *Stupid!* Perhaps she had a point. Later that day, my mom came home from work and went straight to my room and asked a question that instantly reinvigorated me. She said, "Baby, what made you think you could fly?"

Then it hit me. It wasn't the cape or the boots. It wasn't the *S* on my shirt that made me leap. It was the personal sense of significance. I mattered. I was here for a reason. Even though my flying didn't succeed, my worth did. I knew that I was supposed to help people; however, at the age of ten, the only way I could imagine that was to transform into a super-hero. At that early stage I accepted the fact that I was born to do what no one else could but that no superhuman ability was required. All I had to be was myself.

We are all created with purpose. We do not have to spend the precious years that we have trying to find it, because we already have it. We were not created to discover our purpose; we were created because we have purpose. *Not one* of the more than 7.7 billion people on this planet is here by acci-dent. Until we realize that purpose, our existence can lack meaning, but once we comprehend our importance, then we must take the next step to use what we have to make our highest contribution to the world.

My lived experience of understanding my purpose was and still is filled with perils, pitfalls, plateaus, and promises. The internal benchmark that indicates personal fulfillment and the sense of a positive direction is difficult to navigate at times. So we leap incorrectly, attempting to do what we are not born to do. Then we allow our bruises and scars to be-come our identities instead of part of our histories. Navigat-ing through the meandering twists of life's trials requires help and truth.

I want to help alleviate the poverty of satisfaction by tell-ing you my truth. Regardless of what you've been through, your purpose is still an essential part of you. Regardless of how broken you have become, your purpose is still intact. You have something important to offer to the world, and you don't need to be superhuman to make your contribution. All you have to be is yourself. Purpose is not what you do; purpose is who you are. Plans change, but purpose is permanent. Purpose is your superpower.

May we all leap into it.

CHAPTER ELEVEN

Right Turns

I want to be remembered as someone who
used herself and anything she could touch
to work for justice and freedom.
—DOROTHY I. HEIGHT

I remember standing at the intersection of grief and gratitude as I reflected on how far I had come. The longing that
I held as a little boy to help people live better never left me.
Years removed from the events that almost derailed my life, I
sat at my executive desk feeling lost again. I had a criminal
history, but without any criminal record I was able to climb
up the corporate ladder in the automobile industry. I had a
wife, two beautiful children, and a sprawling home. As grateful as I was for where I had landed, there was grief. I was in

the perfect bubble living in the Midwest, insulated from all the unpleasant experiences that I'd become accustomed to. On this particular day, my emotional bubble burst.

The inescapable mingling of joy and pain was familiar along my journey, but in this moment those emotions were prompting me to make a choice. I had mostly stopped talking about my past because I believed, at least on a subconscious level, that I didn't want anyone else to know that I was once in a dark place. Consciously, I knew that something was missing from my life. I carried the feeling of culpability for too long, which left little to no room for me to pick up intentionality and the cause of caring for someone else. As humans we all carry shame, but I think that shame is prolonged when we refuse to admit our contradictions. We choose to cover them up without embracing the notion that we can be flawed and favored at the same time. Shame is not inherent, though; it is inferiority projected onto us by others. I was feeling unworthy because of my history, and the unconscious cover-up of my shame was potentially worse than my crimes. I was set to live my life while I passed my pain along to another generation.

Who wants to live his life as the part posing as the whole? That's how I felt: incomplete, disingenuous, and disoriented. It wasn't enough for me to be personally free. I needed to confront the harmful systems that were complicit in my trauma, knowing that others were still in harm's way. My redemption story needed both freedom in my personal life and freedom from unjust systems. Yes, I went through great suffering—many of us do—but I was transformed by great love, and not everyone experiences that.

I didn't want to respond to an awakening with a cultural reaction. This was a moment of clarity, and it wasn't about me. I could no longer be selfish with the love and hope I was given. A range of questions raced through my mind, and among them this question was the most significant: What responsibility did I bear for the structural injustice that I saw? I could not in good conscience ignore the moral obligation to do more for humanity. Our humanity is inextricably linked; how can it not be? Standing in my office with a suit and tie on, the powerful realization of the deep connection we have as human beings became evident through the emotions that were spilling out.

Much of what I thought was anger in my younger years was really sadness.

I realized it that day because of the sadness that I felt not for myself but for the thousands upon thousands who might be suffering like I used to. I was grieving for them. Grief permits us to accept the world's sorrow without searching for culprits or victims and to recognize the awful truth that all sides are caught up in it. I was falling into the lull of my natural arc of life and my own self-interests, forgetting that I was once lonely, tired, and afraid. Similarly, I was caught up in the difficulties of my past. At some point in our lives we can find ourselves on the side of being either the victim or the culprit, and regardless of which position we're in, we typically are preoccupied with our own preferences. It's when we come to the crossroads that we have to stop, and in that brief moment of pause, we see that we are not the only people who are hurting. On this unusual day I came to that crossroads.

This same day just happened to be the moment I had been waiting for in my career. The president of our company flew in to offer me an executive vice president position with the responsibility of opening a franchise out west. The offer was magnificent. I asked if I could have the night to think it over because I was still wrestling with the sadness of not laboring for others. As I watched the clock slowly wind toward the morning, I stood still and began to intercede for the helpless. Compassion overwhelmed me. My heart and my mind were submerged in a passion to help people live better lives.

I made a conscious choice.

The next morning I walked into my boss's office to inform him that I could not accept the promotion and that I was leaving to start a social enterprise and a church. He thought I was crazy. Maybe I was, but I knew I was making the right turn toward helping others. Consciousness, desire, and intentionality are all paramount; they can build or destroy lives. I could no longer afford to lease space for any type of hatred, hurt, or negativity in my emotional real estate. I intentionally chose to spend the rest of my life being a peacemaker, which first began in my heart and mind. My boss asked me how I was going to fund all of this.

"I'm not sure," was my immediate response, "but I have hope."

He stood up in his meticulously tailored suit that appeared like he had it sewn onto his body and said, "Hope is not a strategy."

"Yes," I replied. "But hope is collateral."

Hope lives at the intersection of faith and love.

Hope is not tied to any future outcome because it survives in the present. It is the collateral of dreams and the consequence of positive intentionality. Hope produces a moral imagination that says the world can be a better place. This is where I had to begin. Realizing that the reality of our times is exceptionally painful to confront, difficult to comprehend, and perplexing to live with, I chose to activate my hope and give it to others. I chose to stand in the middle of the crossroads and meet others at their points of pain.

I often used to feel like I pulled people into my negative world when I was dealing with all my trauma. Sometimes strangers would approach me to say they were interceding for me. I never understood why a person I had no relationship with would have the guts to say that to a complete stranger until I stood in my boss's office explaining to him why I had to leave. I could offer him no logical answer because I was seeking to become an answer. I was willing to stand in the gap of pain and joy, to be a guide for those who are lost, and to be a bridge for those that could not access possibility.

I didn't have the words, but I had the will to try.

In writing about Saint Francis, Richard Rohr described what I was feeling in this way: "We cannot change the world except insofar as we have changed ourselves. We can only give away who we are. We can only offer to others what God has done in us. We have no real mental or logical answers. We must *be* an answer." The seemingly small transformation that I experienced compared to the vastness of the problems of society did not make me second-guess my decision. If what transpired in my life was true, then everything could move from there.

I left my plush executive job to offer to others what had been done for me, to save as many as I could through my story of redemption and by any means necessary. Our stories, our faith, our hope, and our love are extremely contagious because we are deeply connected. When we have the ability to understand how connected we are, we unwrap the gift of knowing that ultimately we decide what our society looks like. To live that truth means we realize that no one on this planet is insignificant. My decisions impact your world, and your choices impact mine.

I know that sounds spooky; in fact, Albert Einstein called this entanglement in the universe "spooky actions at a distance." In the realm of quantum physics, it seems that in every entangled pair of particles, one particle appears to know what is going on with the other, despite the fact that they are frequently separated by extreme distances and there is no known way for such information to be conveyed between them. If your brain starts to ooze out from this observation, don't worry. All it means is that everything is connected. That's why a stranger can say, "I'm interceding for you" or "I'm advocating for you." We can impact people's lives just by letting them know we see them. To stand in the gap for another doesn't require having all the details of her personal situation. Empathy doesn't need details; it needs only a mirror. We can see the face of the other person struggling in our reflection.

My story is your story, and your story is mine.

Like the universe we live in, we are in relationship with one another regardless of race, gender, tribe, or creed. If we choose to live in the realness of our humanity, we can reorder our society and even reshape our world.

I was deeply concerned about issues of pressing importance: poverty, education inequity and inequality, racism, racial disparity, and violence, just to name a few. I joined the array of individuals who were on a similar journey to discover how we can overcome the social barriers that have been in our way for generations. I served on all types of boards, learned to advocate through policy, built organizations, and partnered with a host of entities all for the sake of creating social change. Through all my years of advocacy, preaching, and public service, the one thing that remains a consistent reality is this:

Structural change cannot take place without individual action.

Institutional injustice is very complicated, with many causes and no simple answers. I use the terms *institutional* and *structural injustice* interchangeably because for injustice to continue to exist in any form, it requires an institution to carry out the will of individuals. Structural or institutional injustice is "the disempowerment of members of particular social groups resulting from the subjection to formal and informal rules that systematically thwart their access to resources, opportunities, offices and social positions normally available to other groups."

However, the distinguishing trait of structural injustice reveals that individuals' prejudiced views or evil deeds, even though such prejudice and hatred undeniably exist, are not the sustainable cause. Still, it is the actions of ordinary individuals that perpetuate institutional injustice. The benign neglect of another person's plight leaks into our social practice, social policies, and social institutions. We all have a social role that we play. We are employers and employees. We are citizens, friends, relatives, parents, colleagues, congregants, and neighbors. Our social roles are the expectations, commitments, and actions that we exhibit every day and display under certain circumstances. Each of us assumes a variety of roles throughout our lives. This is where institution and individual action intersect.

For example, parents hoping to have their child attend the best school in their district can be completely unaware of how that one desire can unintentionally perpetuate segregation just as much as the intentional act of a biased homeowner who won't sell his property to someone who doesn't look like him. The racism of the homeowner is not enough to stop people of a different race from moving in; only a law can prevent that from happening perpetually. There was a time when that practice was legal and prevailed in our culture, but individual action changed the law, and individual practice changed culture. Consequently today, it is not legal to discriminate even if you hold those feelings as an individual. On the other hand, the parents who just want what's best for their child and don't have one racist bone in their bodies continue to participate in the practice of a long-standing policy failure that consigns parents and children of a different social class or race to schools that persistently put their children behind.

Iris Marion Young, a prolific thought leader on this subject, observed, "The unintended consequences of the confluence of many actions often produce and reinforce opportunities and constraints, and these often make their mark on the physical conditions of future actions, as well as on the habits and expectations" of others. Due to this "mutually reinforcing" dynamic, it is difficult to change individuals' social positions and the way they influence individuals' lives.

If we just continue to look at our education system from this vantage point, then it becomes easier to understand why it continues to promote residential assignment, meaning that you cannot access certain schools if you don't live in that zip code. Meanwhile, parents who want their child to attend the best school in the district but don't have the address to match can be arrested if they use a different address for that purpose. This is not just an example; it's a reality for many parents seeking the best educational options for their children. "Structural injustices are harms that come to people as a result of structural processes in which many people participate."

How can trying to help your child access a better school be a crime? Yet it is. Just a decade ago—2011, not 1960—a mother living in Akron, Ohio, was arrested for using her father's address, which was in the correct zip code, to enroll her two daughters in a better school. The state called this action "boundary hopping." The mother was initially sentenced to five years but ultimately served only ten days.

In this one scenario, the social role of a parent looking to provide something better for her children caused her to interface with two institutions: education and the criminal justice system. Which brings me to the complexity of structural or institutional injustice. Our structural systems are interlocked. They coexist and mutually strengthen one another. As a result, we cannot solve the problems in one system without also tackling the problems in another.

Here is another way to understand the complexity. The human body is incredible. It contains trillions of cells, seventy-eight different organs, and almost one hundred thousand miles of blood vessels if you stretched them end to end. Amazingly, all of these cells, organs, and vessels work together to keep us alive. If our body systems rely on each other to work well, what about our social systems? Much like our bodies, there is a reciprocal relationship among our social systems. Our systems of housing, education, justice, economics, and health—they are all intertwined.

The majority of our social institutions were started at a time when the intentional subjugation and a fear of people were cultural norms. This wasn't the action of one nefarious person but rather the actions of many individuals. There may have been no personal liability for harmful laws and practices, but there is always a responsibility for them. People voted and fought in wars to either change or keep some of our institutional habits. This is where we can all answer the question of how our actions can produce social and structural change. Responsibility requires action. However, the more institutions and structures are perceived to impact people's decisions, the less agency people think they have.

It will never be up to our institutions to change. It will always be up to us.

This is not an attempt to get us to try to execute as individuals what we are not capable of; rather it is to show that when we take collective action, we can transform our institutions, our policies, and our society. The only way to undo the decisions that cause irreparable harm systemically is to make new decisions. That cannot happen until we face our history. We have to be honest about our past to move forward.

The experiences that caused me the most harm and offered the most hope were in the institutions of education, criminal justice, and faith. The individuals in those institutions who could see me with empathy became the catalysts in helping to transform my life. As a society we ought to be in the business of transforming individuals, not punishing them for their wrong turns or for our selfish predilections. What would happen if we really made just one of our institutions work for the benefit of all? For instance, if we chose to really deliver on the promise of education, we could transcend other institutions as well. Housing and criminal justice systems would begin to transform simultaneously. I'm not suggesting that it's easy. It would truly take collective action and faith to do it, but possibility is not our problem.

The problem is belief.

We collectively believe that our education system is broken. That is the story that we hear and continue to perpetuate rather than understanding that the American education system is working as it was intended. I believed that education was broken, too, and that belief informed my practice when I became a parent. When I sent my son to kindergarten, my consternation was high. I suppose most parents feel this way, but for me it was triggering. Would he suffer what I suffered, could his teachers see his potential, or would inequity persist in another generation? I concluded, based on where we lived, that these questions could not be answered by the public options that were available to us at the time. So we invested in another educational opportunity for him: private school. In third grade he had the chance to dress up as Thurgood Marshall and was encouraged to put the words of Langston Hughes' poem "Dreams" to music. His teacher had noticed his ability to put pen to paper and words to music, so she kept him after school to cultivate his gift. I sat in the audience of the assembly amazed at my son's natural ability to speak publicly and display his aptitude without trepidation.

Mirrored in my son's educational journey is the image I carried in my mind for my own education. He would go to Harvard; I ended up in jail. The polarity of our experiences is a powerful description of not only what our education system is but also what it can be. The fear that I had sending my son to public school was the same fear that can be found in the genesis of our education system. From the very beginning the structure of the education system wasn't broad enough to shoulder the potential and brilliance of all children.

Unfortunately our system was cast from a compulsory model and built from the branches of frail policies instead of by the roots of moral clarity. Its original design was not suitable to educate all children or sustainable to equalize the conditions of social imbalance. Consequently, our education system and policies remain a receptacle for the fears of the individuals that created it and a harbinger for the status quo.

In America, "before the 1830s, education was largely an 'informal, local matter,' in which Catholic, Protestant, and other schools competed for pupils." Aid to schools was unsystematic and provided by local governments, but back then there was no concept of public schools. "The distinction between private and public schools was not crystallized until the 'school wars' of the 1840s, which officially ended the use of public funds to support Catholic schools." The shift from private to public education was a response to a "huge influx of poor, non-Protestant immigrants," most of whom were Irish Catholic. This ushered in the common-school era led by individuals who feared that "whoever controls the schools will control the next generation." So they formed a system out of the steam of the industrial revolution and wrapped it in a one-size-fits-all frame that reflected the beliefs of individuals who prioritized easy over excellence. This allowed segregation and inequity to remain for years, even until today, because they were built into the foundation.

That is part of our history, but it does not have to be our destiny.

More is possible today than ever before, but it takes faith to uproot. It takes hope to rebuild, and we must do it for the benefit of future generations. All the change we are looking for, regardless of the institutions we are trying to impact or the problems we are trying to solve, begins with us as individuals. We cannot turn toward others until we turn toward ourselves. Then and only then can we turn toward the structural injustices that are endemic in our society.

I have driven down many wrong lanes in my life. I have also made some very important right turns. But now I am making another turn, and I'm hoping that you will join me. If the past few years have taught us anything, they have shown that we are responsible for each other. So I'm making a decision to turn toward the helpless and the hurting once again. It is a decision to accept that we as humans are flawed yet powerful. It is a decision to stop asking what I can do and take a look at what I am doing. To devote myself to serving others and doing my absolute best to ensure that future generations don't inherit my adverse experiences. It is a decision to be used up and to spend every ounce of my potential to improve the world. It is a decision to stop running from my past and use my story to build hope in other human beings. It is a decision to be fully present in this precious moment.

I turn intentionally toward you.

Epilogue

While the tale of how we suffer, and how we are
delighted, and how we may triumph is never new,
it always must be heard. There isn't any other tale to tell,
it's the only light we've got in all this darkness.
—JAMES BALDWIN in "Sonny's Blues"

We all have our own tales to tell. We all have our own personal journeys full of raw material like the kind James Baldwin wrote about. These exist inside the confines of a bigger story, a collective story. *Our* story.

Our story consists of those dynamics that shape and affect us but are larger than ourselves. These include the colors of our skins, the health of our communities, the characters of our families. They include our churches, our cultures. These places are our training grounds, the places where we learn to trust and where we find a sense of belonging. Our story is where we develop unconditional love. But too many times we become so deafened by our environment that we never open our ears to hear anything else. Instead, we defend our culture and remain wrapped up in our individual narratives. Both the individual story and our collective story are interwoven throughout the narrative. Both are venues for intervention and action.

Yet there is a greater story even still. This is *the* story. It resides beyond individual tale and collective history. It is the pathos that fills our hearts when we see or hear the pain of people who may look different but whose difficulties are not foreign to us. It's the road we all travel when we see a way to bypass the opportunity for societal and systemic change but simply refuse to take it. The truth of the story is this: we are all human, and we have much power, if we choose to use it, to decide how our society looks. The only way change can happen is for us to take a giant turn from our present direction and drive toward the story. The story is the highway to a better place. It is the road that holds all the signs of our realities and says that we can do something about them. We have incredible power to choose our future and create a culture of possibility instead of a culture of punishment.

The key to—and genesis of—a culture of possibility is to unlock individual purpose, to know that every individual has a God-given purpose and decide as a society not to leave anyone trapped inside personal pain. This frees us from our own private worlds and tiny cultures. It is intentionally moving beyond talking toward action. Conversations are wonderful, and we need to continue to have them. But when will change come? It will come only when we collectively listen to each other, refuse to jump to conclusions without self-reflection, and choose to truly reconstruct a society that's equitable and just for all. A society that makes a U-turn.

If we're not willing to turn around toward a neighbor with a different story, toward a colleague with a different opinion, or toward an opponent with a different affiliation and see his humanity, our very lives lie hanging in the balance.

There is a path to purpose and a culture of possibility, but it requires that we turn toward one another.

Will you join me?

Discussion Questions

Prologue

1. At a teacher appreciation dinner, Michael Phillips asks the CEO of city schools the following question: "What would it look like if somebody intentionally took on some of your lowest-performing schools with the intention of turning them around? What if they created a network among those schools? What would that look like in partnership with the district?"

2. What would it look like to do that in your city or town? How could you become involved with that?

3. In 1993, Michael Phillips found himself at a chaotic intersection in his life. A phone call from his mother changed that story. Have you found yourself at a dramatic moment where you decided or were forced to make a change? What did that look like?

Chapter One: My Soul Looks Back and Wonders

1. Did someone in your childhood ever attempt to crush your dreams? Who was it and how did you react to this?

2. Thurgood Marshall said, "A man can make what he wants of himself if he truly believes that he must be ready for hard work and many heartbreaks." What do you think when you hear this quote?

3. Have you ever experienced redlining in your life? Have you been impacted by an invisible line determining where you live or go to school or work? Do you feel separated by a wall where people on the other side of the fence tell you that your dreams are invalid?

4. "I believe every person has genius inside him," Michael Phillips writes. What does that phrase mean to you?

Chapter Two: The Predator and the Prey

1. Have the stereotypes that label Blacks, particularly Black males, as "brutes" or criminals, as lewd, hypersexual, or predatory, changed over the years, or have they been heightened in the recent events of the last few years?

2. Growing up, Phillips sees many of his friends changing and dying, as if they were all "being sifted like wheat but we were only the chaff." Young lives pulled into darkness and living in fear only to turn to aggression to cope with the hopelessness they saw. Have you witnessed people in

your own life pulled into this darkness and unable to find hope?

3. Richard Phillips told his son, "Nobody else has your fingerprint, Michael. Nobody else has your purpose." He believed that despite the limited view for opportunity, possibility still remained. Do you believe this? Do you see something bigger and better out there?

Chapter Three: How Are the Children?

1. Statistics say one in seven children in the US lives in poverty, and approximately 73 percent of children living in poverty are children of color. School shootings and daily gun violence are a never-ending epidemic. Our juvenile justice system tries kids as adults as young as thirteen years old. How have we allowed ourselves to become this way?

2. Have you seen a paradox of survivorship in others around you or even in yourself? Times when parents verbalize fear-based survival messages and pass them along to their children and grandchildren? Do you hear comments like "Don't ask for help" or "It's dangerous out there?" How can you change the message that initially helped the oppressed stay safe?

3. As Michael Phillips's father told him, "You're going to get detractors confronting you about what you want to accomplish and do, so you have to know that you know that you know that you know, because no one else is going to

know that for you." How did you end up knowing that you know that you know? Who came along at an early age to help make this happen?

Chapter Four: Bitter Seed

1. What do you think of the familiar passage in Job that says, "The Lord gives and the Lord takes away"? How has this looked in your own life?
2. Phillips writes, "Grief is not a single emotion. Nor is it a single event. Grief is a cycle. When we have loss enter our lives, we can feel displaced." Has grief ever made you feel displaced in your own life? How did you deal with it?
3. After his father's death, Phillips chose to live in two worlds—his father's world of faith and the secular world. He used both of them for his pain. Have you ever found yourself doing this, living two different lives in two different worlds?
4. Have you ever mistook God's silence for His absence?
5. Do you believe Frederick Douglas when he said, "It is easier to build strong children than to repair broken men"?
6. After moving to the suburbs, Phillips felt like he was living in a foreign country. Have you ever experienced this feeling of being the "only"? How did you cope with that?

Chapter Five: Walking Without Purpose

1. "You see us as you want to see us—in the simplest terms, in the most convenient definitions." This quote from *The Breakfast Club* accurately depicts how society can falsely sum up people in the most elementary ways. How did people see you growing up? What was your identity and how did you deal with it?

2. Athletics gave Phillips his first glimpse of a path, a place of hope that he could pursue. Did you find a place or a purpose like this during your childhood?

3. Phillips poses this question: "Can public education in its current form be a revolutionary agent for change? Or must it be an agent only of repeating the same patterns that have brought us to the difficulties and inequities of our present day?" What are your thoughts on this?

4. What are your thoughts when someone says, "I don't see color"?

Chapter Six: Crash

1. Heading to college, Phillips says, "I was neither a problem to be solved nor a broken individual to be fixed. I was a young Black male who wanted to learn." Yet growing up, he believed he wouldn't graduate school and that he would either end up in jail or die on the streets. He knew he needed to contend with the negative typecast heard so

often. How have you or others in your life dealt with these deficit narratives?

2. How do we battle biases and false statistics that say things like "there are more Black males in a cell than there are in college" or that "overwhelmingly, Black fathers are absent"? How can we shift others' expectations or even biases in ourselves?

3. When difficult times have come into your life, how have you dealt with them? Do you feel like we also have hope in the midst of life's havoc? Do you believe we always have an advocate even when we feel alone?

Chapter Seven: Short Money

1. Phillips discusses the concept of the pedagogy of poverty. He states that "the instructional practices were skewed more toward dumping information and enforcing behavior than toward providing opportunities for students to raise questions, make sense of the environment, and address challenges in their families and beyond." Do you see this as still happening today in schools?

2. The environment Phillips was in taught him that school didn't offer purpose, and that if you had money, you had power. What sort of things does your environment teach you?

3. The addict Phillips met tells him, "We are all on something.

We are all addicted to something." What things can we be addicted to other than drugs and alcohol?

Chapter Eight: Tragedy Interrupted

1. Phillips writes that "the underbelly of criminal justice is ugly" and that our culture needs to produce villains in order to function. Do you feel we've created a culture of punishment? How do we change this?
2. What are the alternatives to incarceration? What are ways where the justice system can be changed?
3. In prison, Phillips found himself with plenty of time to think, forced to face himself and realize why he was there. Have you ever been at a point in your life when you were forced to do the same thing? What was the outcome?
4. "It is not our experiences that make or break us. It's our interpretations of them that ultimately make the difference." What do you think about Phillips's statement?
5. Have you ever seen potential in someone else who didn't believe they had any? How did you help them see this?

Chapter Nine: Redemption and Reentry

1. "More than ten thousand individuals are released each week from state and federal prisons," Phillips writes. "We say that once people leave prison, they have paid their

debts to society, but in actuality we burden them by placing their criminality in the luggage that they carry for a
lifetime." He discusses ways to combat this, things such as
meaningful work environments, effective coping strategies,
positive social engagement, positive relationships, and
healthy thinking patterns. What are the ways we can individually help former convicts let go of the luggage they
carry?

2. Have you ever been at a place in your life where you felt as
though you didn't measure up to a place or a person, much
like Phillips felt when he went to ORU?

3. What does it mean when Phillips says, "Deliverance is not
freedom; deliverance is preparation for freedom"?

4. Have you ever asked God what He wants from you? Have
you ever been at a place like Phillips was at ORU when he
had an encounter with God?

Chapter Ten: No Success Without Struggle

1. "Our systems of education, justice, health, economics, and
government have become the hotbed for ostracized people." So what is our societal story?

2. How can we get more people access to a sense of purpose
and a high-quality education?

3. What does systemic change mean to you?

4. What does it mean to have the ears to hear and the will to
talk about it in order to interrupt tragedies in other peo-

ple's lives? Do you have the moral courage to do things differently in order to create right turns from wrong lanes?

5. What is the purpose in your life? Who or what has helped you see and foster this?

Chapter Eleven: Right Turns

1. "Grief permits us to accept the world's sorrow without searching for culprits or victims." Do you find yourself preoccupied with one of these two sides?

2. Phillips says that hope is collateral. What does this mean to you?

3. "Structural change cannot take place without individual action." How can we take action in today's world to make an impact?

4. To effect long-term social transformation in how we react to crime or violence, communities should begin carefully analyzing the underlying causes that have resulted in violent or repressive situations for disadvantaged groups. Here are several transformative questions we should be asking:

- How can we develop our personal and communal capacity to react to trauma in a transformative manner and to promote accountability?
- How can we rebalance power in the direction of communal liberation?

- How can we create resilient and life-affirming movements that are successful and sustainable?
- How can we alter our reaction to violence in such a way that we protect survivors and their right to self-determination while also assisting individuals in fundamentally changing their abusive behaviors?

5. In order to effect systemic change, you are more than likely going to have to make some uncomfortable turns toward other people's perspectives and ideas, but, most important, you are going to have to change too—and that's always difficult. Are you willing to change to make change happen?

Further Reading

Alexander, Michelle. *The New Jim Crow: Mass Incarceration in the Age of Colorblindness*. New York: The New Press, 2020.

Wilkerson, Isabel. *Caste: The Origin of Our Discontents*. New York: Random House, 2020.

Rothstein, Richard. *The Color of Law: A Forgotten History of How Our Government Segregated America*. New York: Liveright, 2017.

Stevenson, Bryan. *Just Mercy: A Story of Justice and Redemption*. New York: One World, 2014.

Tatum, Beverly Daniel. *Why Are All the Black Kids Sitting Together in the Cafeteria?: And Other Conversations About Race*. New York: Basic, 2017.

Sandel, Michael J. *Justice: What's the Right Thing to Do?* New York: Farrar, Straus and Giroux, 2009.

Heather McGhee. *The Sum of Us: What Racism Costs Everyone and How We Can Prosper Together*. New York: One World, 2021.

Meacham, Jon. *The Soul of America: The Battle of Our Better Angels.* New York: Random House, 2018.

Menakem, Resmaa. *My Grandmother's Hands: Racialized Trauma and the Pathway to Mending Our Hearts and Bodies.* Las Vegas: Central Recovery Press, 2017.

Acknowledgments

To Anita, Michael, and Olivia, my wife and children. Thank you for listening to me read and labor over every word, for your helpful feedback and willingness to give all of your support.

To Bishop T. D. Jakes. Thank you for your encouragement and guidance.

To my mom, Sandra Phillips-Hayden. Thank you for never giving up on me.

Notes

Prologue

x   **"Seven public elementary school programs"**: Bowie State University, "Partnerships Expand Impact of Education Programs," https://bowiestate .edu/about/administration-and-governance/office-of-the-president/reports /2020-annual-report/academics/index.php. See also the National Assessment of Educational Progress (NAEP) statistics.

Chapter One: My Soul Looks Back and Wonders

3   **"Hold fast to dreams"**: Langston Hughes, "Dreams," in *The Collected Works of Langston Hughes,* ed. Arnold Lampersad, vol. 1, *The Poems: 1921–1940* (Columbia, MO: University of Missouri Press, 2001), 154.

6   **"Equal means getting the same thing"**: "Meet the Legal Team Behind Brown v. Board of Education," NAACP Legal Defense and Educational Fund, www.naacpldf.org/ldf-celebrates-60th-anniversary-brown-v-board -education/meet-legal-minds-behind-brown-v-board-education.

6   **"A man can make what he wants"**: "Quotes," Thurgood Marshall, thurgoodmarshall.com/quotes-by-thurgood-marshall.

9   **"What is the quality of your intent?"**: Biography.com editors, "9 Powerful Quotes by Thurgood Marshall," Biography.com, A&E Television Networks, January 28, 2021, www.biography.com/news/thurgood -marshall-quotes.

13 **The studies show**: Robin Chait, *Removing Chronically Ineffective Teachers: Barriers and Opportunities* (Washington, DC: Center for American Progress, 2010), 1–4, https://cdn.americanprogress.org/wp -content/uploads/issues/2010/03/pdf/teacher_dismissal.pdf.

13 **"a positive link"**: Linda Darling-Hammond, Marla E. Hyler, and

Madelyn Gardner, "Effective Teacher Professional Development," Learning Policy Institute, June 5, 2017, https://learningpolicyinstitute .org/product/effective-teacher-professional-development-report.

15　**President Barack Obama said:** "President Obama's Remarks to the Hispanic Chamber of Commerce," transcript, *New York Times,* March 10, 2009, www.nytimes.com/2009/03/10/us/politics/10text-obama.html.

15　**The etymology of the word** *educate*: *Online Etymology Dictionary,* s.v. "educate," www.etymonline.com/word/educate.

16　**not allowing kids to be tested for giftedness:** "System Failure: Gifted Education in the United States," Gifted Education Research and Resource Institute, Purdue University, www.education.purdue.edu/geri /new-publications/gifted-education-in-the-united-states.

16　**"Be fruitful":** Genesis 1:28.

19　**"None of us got where":** Biography.com editors, "9 Powerful Quotes."

20　**I was in a declining school system:** *Urban Schools: The Challenge of Location and Poverty,* National Center for Education Statistics, https://nces.ed.gov/pubs/96184all.pdf; "Comprehensive Support and Improvement," California Department of Education, www.cde.ca.gov /sp/sw/t1/csi.asp.

21　**"The educational foundations of our society":** National Commission on Excellence in Education, *A Nation at Risk: The Imperative for Educational Reform* (Washington, DC: US Government Printing Office, 1983), https://edreform.com/wp-content/uploads/2013/02/A_Nation _At_Risk_1983.pdf.

21　**"open letter":** National Commission on Excellence, *Nation at Risk.*

22　**Despite the Supreme Court's landmark decision:** History.com editors, "Brown v. Board of Education," History, May 13, 2021, www.history .com/topics/black-history/brown-v-board-of-education-of-topeka.

22　**"more than half of the nation's schoolchildren":** Sarah Mervosh, "How Much Wealthier Are White School Districts Than Nonwhite Ones? $23 Billion Dollars, Report Says," *New York Times,* February 27, 2019, www.nytimes.com/2019/02/27/education/school-districts-funding-white -minorities.html.

23　**"The nexus":** Keith Meatto, "Still Separate, Still Unequal: Teaching about School Segregation and Educational Inequality," *New York Times,* May 2, 2019, www.nytimes.com/2019/05/02/learning/lesson -plans/still-separate-still-unequal-teaching-about-school-segregation-and -educational-inequality.html.

23　**receive $23 billion less:** Mervosh, "How Much Wealthier."

23　*Brown* **had the tragic effect:** Madeline Will, "65 Years After 'Brown v. Board,' Where Are All the Black Educators?," *Education Week,* May 14, 2019, www.edweek.org/policy-politics/65-years-after-brown-v-board -where-are-all-the-black-educators/2019/05.

23   "After the decision": Will, "65 Years After 'Brown v. Board.'"

24   "a growing body of research": Will, "65 Years After 'Brown v. Board.'"

24   A 2017 Johns Hopkins study: Johns Hopkins University, "With Just One Black Teacher, Black Students More Likely to Graduate," news release, April 5, 2017, https://releases.jhu.edu/2017/04/05/with-just -one-black-teacher-black-students-more-likely-to-graduate.

24   "less likely to be suspended, expelled, or placed in detention": Evie Blad, "Black Students Less Likely to Be Disciplined by Black Teachers, Study Says," *Education Week,* November 1, 2016, www.edweek.org /leadership/black-students-less-likely-to-be-disciplined-by-black-teachers -study-says/2016/11.

24   accepted in gifted-education classes: Indiana University Bloomington, "Study: Black Students More Likely to Be Identified as Gifted if Teachers Are Black," news release, May 10, 2016, https://archive.news.indiana .edu/releases/iu/2016/05/gifted-student-placement.shtml.

24   Black instructors' expectations: Jill Rosen, "Teacher Expectations Reflect Racial Biases, Johns Hopkins Study Suggests," *The Hub,* March 30, 2016, https://hub.jhu.edu/2016/03/30/racial-bias-teacher-expectations -black-white.

25   "removes or excludes a student": "The Pathway from Exclusionary Discipline to the School to Prison Pipeline," American Psychological Association Services, www.apa.org/advocacy/health-disparities/discipline -facts.pdf.

25   "disparities in the use": "Pathway from Exclusionary Discipline."

26   "children thrive academically, behaviorally": *Maryland Commission on the School-to-Prison Pipeline and Restorative Practices,* December 20, 2018, 7, www.law.umaryland.edu/media/SOL/pdfs/Programs/ADR /STPP%20%20RP%20Commission%20Final%20Report.pdf.

26   approximately 79 percent of public school teachers: Institute of Education Sciences, *Characteristics of Public and Private Elementary and Secondary School Teachers in the United States: Results From the 2017–18 National Teacher and Principal Survey* (Washington, DC: U.S. Department of Education, 2020), https://nces.ed.gov/pubs2020/2020142.pdf.

26   "slightly more than half": Madeline Will, "Still Mostly White and Female: New Federal Data on the Teaching Profession," *Education Week,* April 14, 2020, www.edweek.org/leadership/still-mostly-white-and-female -new-federal-data-on-the-teaching-profession/2020/04.

26   the old gospel hymn: Mahalia Jackson, "How I Got Over," by Clara Ward, *How I Got Over,* Columbia, 1976, https://genius.com/Mahalia -jackson-how-i-got-over-live-lyrics.

Notes

Chapter Two: The Predator and the Prey

27 **"It's like a jungle sometimes":** Grandmaster Flash and the Furious Five, "The Message," *The Message,* Sugar Hill Records, 1982, https://www .songfacts.com/lyrics/grandmaster-flash-the-furious-five/the-message.

31 **War on Drugs:** History.com editors, "War on Drugs," History.com, A&E Television Networks, December 17, 2019, www.history.com/topics/crime /the-war-on-drugs.

31 **Federal funding was split:** White House Office of National Drug Control Policy, *National Drug Control Strategy* (Washington, DC: U.S. Government Printing Office, 1990), 100, www.ojp.gov/pdffiles1/ondcp /121637.pdf.

31 **treatment-on-demand approach:** Michael Tonry, "Race and the War on Drugs," *University of Chicago Legal Forum* 1994, no. 1, art. 4, 25, https://chicagounbound.uchicago.edu/cgi/viewcontent.cgi?article=1155 &context=uclf.

31 **"During the 1980s, Congress created":** "Federal Drug Sentencing Laws Bring High Cost, Low Return," Pew Charitable Trusts, August 27, 2015, www.pewtrusts.org/en/research-and-analysis/issue-briefs/2015/08 /federal-drug-sentencing-laws-bring-high-cost-low-return.

34 **Noted criminologist Alfred Blumstein:** Tonry, "Race and the War on Drugs."

35 **well into the 1990s:** "Decades of Disparity: Drug Arrests and Race in the United States," Human Rights Watch, March 2, 2009, www.hrw.org /report/2009/03/02/decades-disparity/drug-arrests-and-race-united-states.

35 **Being male and Black:** Camille Busette, "A New Deal for Poor African-American and Native-American Boys," Brookings, March 14, 2018, www.brookings.edu/blog/fixgov/2018/03/14/a-new-deal-for-poor-african -american-and-native-american-boys.

35 **From education:** Richard V. Reeves, Sarah Nzau, and Ember Smith, "The Challenges Facing Black Men—and the Case for Action," Brookings, November 19, 2020, www.brookings.edu/blog/up-front/2020/11 /19/the-challenges-facing-black-men-and-the-case-for-action.

35 **to low-paying employment:** Fred Dews, "Charts of the Week: Earnings and Unemployment Gaps by Race," Brookings, February 19, 2021, www.brookings.edu/blog/brookings-now/2021/02/19/charts-of-the-week -earnings-and-unemployment-gaps-by-race.

35 **from life expectancy to incarceration:** Reeves, Nzau, and Smith, "Challenges Facing Black Men."

35 **Black men have the highest unemployment:** Reeves, Nzau, and Smith, "Challenges Facing Black Men."

36 **"direct result of centuries":** Busette, "New Deal."

36 **"on labeling blacks"**: Busette, "New Deal."

37 **Black males who graduated**: Emily Badger, "Young Black Men Face Daunting Odds in Life. These Programs Can Help," *Washington Post*, June 3, 2015, www.washingtonpost.com/news/wonk/wp/2015/06/03 /young-black-men-face-daunting-odds-in-life-these-programs-can-help.

38 **Moving to Opportunity (MTO)**: National Bureau of Economic Research, *Moving to Opportunity for Fair Housing Demonstration Program: Final Impacts Evaluation* (Washington, DC: U.S. Department of Housing and Urban Development, 2011), www.huduser.gov/publications /pdf/MTOFHD_fullreport_v2.pdf.

38 **Over 4,600 families from high-poverty areas**: "Evaluating the Impact of Moving to Opportunity in the United States," J-PAL North America, www.povertyactionlab.org/evaluation/evaluating-impact-moving-opportunity -united-states.

39 **"Education is the most powerful weapon"**: Nelson Mandela, "Lighting Your Way to a Better Future" (speech, launch of Mindset Network, Planetarium, University of Witwatersrand, Johannesburg, South Africa, July 16, 2003), http://db.nelsonmandela.org/speeches/pub_view.asp?pg =item&ItemID=NMS909.

42 **"There is nothing like a dream"**: Victor Hugo, *Les Misérables* (New York: Signet Classics, 1987), 641–42.

43 **George Pullman hired thousands of Black men**: History.com editors, "Pullman Porters," History, A&E Television Networks, February 15, 2019, www.history.com/topics/black-history/pullman-porters.

45 **I never saw a wild thing**: D. H. Lawrence, "Self-Pity," in *The Complete Poems of D. H. Lawrence* (Hertfordshire, UK: Wordsworth Poetry Library, 1994), 382.

Chapter Three: How Are the Children?

47 **"No role models"**: J. Cole, "No Role Modelz," *2014 Forest Hills Drive*, Columbia, 2014, https://www.songfacts.com/lyrics/j-cole/no-role-modelz.

47 **"Kasserian Ingera"**: Patrick T. O'Neill, "And How Are the Children?," Unitarian Universalist Association, www.uua.org/worship/words/reading /and-how-are-the-children.

49 **operating under "separate but equal" constraints**: Vanessa Siddle Walker and Kim Nesta Archung, "The Segregated Schooling of Blacks in the Southern United States and South Africa," *Comparative Education Review* 47, no. 1 (February 2003), www.journals.uchicago.edu/doi /full/10.1086/373961.

49 **Black Americans saw education**: Walker and Archung, "Segregated Schooling of Blacks."

49 **Lincoln School:** James P. Kaetz, "Lincoln School," *Encyclopedia of Alabama,* October 31, 2017, www.encyclopediaofalabama.org/article/h-2570.

49 **"for graduating a high proportion":** Wikipedia, s.v. "Lincoln Normal School," May 28, 2021, 18:17, https://en.wikipedia.org/wiki/Lincoln_Normal_School; see also Clifton H. Johnson, "Powerful Little School," *Crisis* 79, no. 5 (May 1972): 156, www.google.com/books/edition/Crisis/kH_XAAAAMAAJ.

50 **Almost one in seven children:** Children's Defense Fund, *The State of America's Children 2021* (Washington, DC: Children's Defense Fund, 2021), 14, 38, www.childrensdefense.org/wp-content/uploads/2021/03/The-State-of-Americas-Children-2021.pdf.

51 **school shootings were occurring:** Lesli Maxwell et al., "School Shootings This Year: How Many and Where," *Education Week,* June 21, 2021, www.edweek.org/leadership/school-shootings-this-year-how-many-and-where/2021/03.

52 **"paradox of survivorship":** Mary Ann Cantrell and Teresa M. Conte, "Between Being Cured and Being Healed: The Paradox of Childhood Cancer Survivorship," *Qualitative Health Research* 19, no. 3 (March 2009), https://journals.sagepub.com/doi/10.1177/1049732308330467.

63 **"The turntables might wobble":** Run-DMC, "Peter Piper," *Raising Hell,* Universal Music, 1986, https://www.songfacts.com/lyrics/run-dmc/peter-piper.

Chapter Four: Bitter Seed

67 **"Everything I ever learned that mattered":** Amy Anderson, "T. D. Jakes Wants You to Suffer," *SUCCESS,* June 12, 2017, www.success.com/td-jakes-wants-you-to-suffer.

68 **In context, Job said those words:** Job 1:20–21.

75 **"Words are things":** Maya Angelou, quoted in Lisa Capretto, "Dr. Maya Angelou on the Power of Words," HuffPost, June 10, 2014, www.huffpost.com/entry/maya-angelou-power-of-words_n_5462077.

77 **"A man can no more diminish":** C. S. Lewis, *The Problem of Pain* (New York: Macmillan, 1962), 53.

81 **increased involvement of school-based law:** "Safe School-Based Enforcement through Collaboration, Understanding, and Respect: Local Implementation Rubric," U.S. Departments of Education and Justice, www2.ed.gov/documents/press-releases/secure-implementation.pdf.

82 **too many schools are focused:** Maryland Commission on the School-to-Prison Pipeline and Restorative Practices, *Final Report and Collaborative Action Plan,* December 29, 2018, 7, www.law.umaryland.edu

/media/SOL/pdfs/Programs/ADR/STPP%20%20RP%20Commission
%20Final%20Report.pdf.

82   **"combination of factors"**: Maryland Commission on the School-to-
      Prison Pipeline, *Final Report*, 22.

82   **innovative learning approaches to discipline**: Maryland Commission on
      the School-to-Prison Pipeline, *Final Report*, 33.

83   **"The Latin roots"**: Maryland Commission on the School-to-Prison
      Pipeline, *Final Report*, 33.

83   **Approximately eight million students**: "School Counselors Matter,"
      The Education Trust, February 1, 2019, https://edtrust.org/resource
      /school-counselors-matter/.

83   **continuum of restorative approaches**: Maryland Commission on the
      School-to-Prison Pipeline, *Final Report*, 46–49.

Chapter Five: Walking Without Purpose

88   **"You see us as you want to see us"**: "Quotes," *The Breakfast Club*, di-
      rected by John Hughes, Universal Pictures, 1985, www.imdb.com/title
      /tt0088847/companycredits?ref_=tt_ql_dt_4.

97   **"our society has socialized us"**: Dorinda Carter Andrews, "The Con-
      sciousness Gap in Education—an Equity Imperative," TEDxLansingED,
      TEDx Talks, March 10, 2014, www.youtube.com/watch?v=iOrgf3w
      TUbo.

97   **"One of the things that I think prevents us"**: Andrews, "Consciousness
      Gap in Education."

97   **Critical consciousness as a social philosophy**: Alexis Jemal, "Critical
      Consciousness: A Critique and Critical Analysis of the Literature," *The
      Urban Review* 49, no. 4 (2017): 602–26, www.ncbi.nlm.nih.gov/pmc
      /articles/PMC5892452.

98   **"Whatever is received into anything"**: Thomas Aquinas, *Summa Theo-
      logiae*, ques. 76, art. 2, www.newadvent.org/summa/1076.htm#article2.

98   **an inspiring, strengths-based, problem-solving approach**: Jemal, "Criti-
      cal Consciousness."

102   **"you have to be a lion"**: Dave Chappelle, "Dave Chappelle Accep-
      tance Speech: 2019 Mark Twain Prize—Transcript," Scraps from the
      Loft, January 13, 2020, https://scrapsfromtheloft.com/2020/01/13/dave
      -chappelle-acceptance-speech-2019-mark-twain-prize.

Chapter Six: Crash

104   **"Turn your wounds into wisdom"**: Oprah Winfrey, "Commencement
      Address" (speech, Wellesley College, Wellesley, MA, May 30, 1997),

www.wellesley.edu/events/commencement/archives/1997commencement
/commencementaddress.

105 **less access to the full variety:** Meredith B. L. Anderson, *A Seat at the Table: African American Youth's Perceptions of K–12 Education* (Washington, DC: United Negro College Fund, 2018), 10, https://cdn.uncf .org/wp-content/uploads/reports/Advocacy_ASATTBro_4-18F_Digital .pdf.

105 **Black youth stated that academic achievement:** Anderson, *Seat at the Table,* 6.

106 **Those implicit associations reside:** Charlotte Ruhl, "Implicit or Unconscious Bias," Simply Psychology, July 1, 2020, www.simplypsychology .org/implicit-bias.html.

107 **about 2.5 million Black dads:** Jo Jones and William D. Mosher, "Fathers' Involvement With Their Children: United States, 2006–2010," *National Health Statistics Reports,* no. 71 (December 20, 2013), www .cdc.gov/nchs/data/nhsr/nhsr071.pdf; see also Josh Levs, "No, Most Black Kids Are Not Fatherless," HuffPost, July 26, 2016, www.huffpost .com/entry/no-most-black-kids-are-no_b_11109876.

107 **more than 1.4 million Black males:** Jenée Desmond-Harris, "The Myth That There Are More Black Men in Prison than in College, Debunked in One Chart," *Vox,* February 12, 2015, www.vox.com/2015/2/12 /8020959/black-men-prison-college.

107 **"Numbers aside":** Desmond-Harris, "Myth That There Are More."

107 **when 38 percent of the prison population:** Ashley Nellis, *The Color of Justice: Racial and Ethnic Disparity in State Prisons* (Washington, DC: The Sentencing Project, 2016), 4, www.sentencingproject.org/wp-content /uploads/2016/06/The-Color-of-Justice-Racial-and-Ethnic-Disparity-in -State-Prisons.pdf.

112 **"Surely I know the plans":** Jeremiah 29:11, NRSV.

114 **"Trust in the LORD":** Proverbs 3:5–6, NRSV.

Chapter Seven: Short Money

118 **"Wherever purpose is not known":** Myles Munroe, *In Pursuit of Purpose: The Legacy and Wisdom of Myles Munroe* (Shippensburg, PA: Destiny Image, 2015), 72.

119 **Fannie Lou Hamer:** Kay Mills, *This Little Light of Mine: The Life of Fannie Lou Hamer* (Lexington, KY: University of Kentucky Press, 2007), 37, 57, www.google.com/books/edition/This_Little_Light_of _Mine/0RGJ9fKIoFwC.

120 **It also triggered:** Ruth Delaney et al., "American History, Race, and Prison," *Reimagining Prison Web Report,* Vera Institute of Justice,

October 2018, www.vera.org/reimagining-prison-web-report/american
-history-race-and-prison.

120   **Newly freed slaves:** Delaney et al., "American History, Race, and Prison."

131   **"Pride goes before destruction":** Proverbs 16:18, NRSV.

135   **"All crime is a kind of disease":** Jag Parvesh Chandler, ed., *Teachings of Mahatma Gandhi* (Lahore: Indian Printing Works, 1945), 145.

Chapter Eight: Tragedy Interrupted

140   **more than six hundred thousand inmates:** "Incarceration and Reentry," Office of the Assistant Secretary for Planning and Evaluation, U.S. Department of Health and Human Services, https://aspe.hhs.gov/incarceration -reentry.

140   **According to the Bureau of Prisons:** Ken Hyle, "Annual Determination of Average Cost of Incarceration Fee (COIF)," Bureau of Prisons, November 19, 2019, www.federalregister.gov/documents/2019/11/19/2019 -24942/annual-determination-of-average-cost-of-incarceration-fee -coif.

151   **"Trauma decontextualized":** Resmaa Menakem, "Notice the Rage, Notice the Silence," June 4, 2020, in *On Being with Krista Tippett*, podcast transcript, https://onbeing.org/programs/resmaa-menakem-notice-the -rage-notice-the-silence.

Chapter Nine: Redemption and Reentry

153   **"Only society make rules":** Bob Marley, quoted in "Bob Marley's Music and Magic Endure," *All Things Considered*, NPR, May 11, 2006, www .npr.org/templates/story/story.php?storyId=5398576.

154   **State and federal criminal history:** *Bureau of Justice Statistics, Survey of State Criminal History Information Systems,* 2018 (Washington, DC: U.S. Department of Justice, 2020), 3, www.ojp.gov/pdffiles1/bjs /grants/255651.pdf.

154   **more than forty thousand legal "collateral consequences":** Chidi Umez and Joshua Gaines, *After the Sentence, More Consequences: A National Report of Barriers to Work* (New York: The Council of State Governments Justice Center, 2021), 3, https://csgjusticecenter.org/publications /after-the-sentence-more-consequences/national-report.

154   **More than ten thousand individuals are released:** "Prisoners and Prison Reentry," U.S. Department of Justice, www.justice.gov/archive/fbci /progmenu_reentry.html.

155 **5-Key Model:** Carrie Davis-Pettus and Stephanie Kennedy, "Researching and Responding to Barriers to Reentry: Early Findings from a Multi-State Trial," Institute for Justice Research and Development, November 2018, 6, https://ijrd.csw.fsu.edu/sites/g/files/upcbnu1766/files/media/images/publication_pdfs/5Key_1st_Report_FINAL_0.pdf.

162 **"How Great Thou Art":** Carl Gustav Boberg, "How Great Thou Art," trans. Stuart K. Hine, 1885, public domain.

167 **"Troubles don't last always":** "I'm So Glad Troubles Don't Last Always," public domain, https://hymnary.org/text/im_so_glad_troubles_dont_last_always.

Chapter Ten: No Success Without Struggle

168 **"What and how much had I lost":** Ralph Ellison, *Invisible Man* (New York: Vintage International, 1995), 266.

171 **The etymology of** *educate*: *Online Etymology Dictionary*, s.v. "educate," www.etymonline.com/word/educate.

171 **The etymology of** *purpose*: *Online Etymology Dictionary*, s.v. "purpose (n.)," www.etymonline.com/word/purpose.

174 **state and municipal investment:** Policy and Program Studies Service, "State and Local Expenditures on Corrections and Education," U.S. Department of Education, July 2016, https://www2.ed.gov/rschstat/eval/other/expenditures-corrections-education/brief.pdf.

174 **From 1989 to 2013:** Policy and Program Studies Service, "State and Local Expenditures."

174 **the total cost per inmate:** Chris Mai and Ram Subramanian, "Prison Spending in 2015," in *The Price of Prisons,* Vera Institute of Justice, May 2017, www.vera.org/publications/price-of-prisons-2015-state-spending-trends/price-of-prisons-2015-state-spending-trends/price-of-prisons-2015-state-spending-trends-prison-spending.

174 **spend $14,840 to educate a child:** Melanie Hanson, "U.S. Public Education Spending Statistics," EducationData.org, April 22, 2021, https://educationdata.org/public-education-spending-statistics.

175 **"Culture is the characteristics and knowledge":** Kim Ann Zimmermann, "What Is Culture?," Live Science, July 12, 2017, www.livescience.com/21478-what-is-culture-definition-of-culture.html.

175 **"patterns of behaviors and interactions":** "What Is Culture?: CARLA's Definition," Center for Advanced Research on Language Acquisition, University of Minnesota, https://carla.umn.edu/culture/definitions.html.

182 **"a stoppage or hindering":** *Merriam-Webster,* s.v. "interruption," www.merriam-webster.com/dictionary/interruption.

Chapter Eleven: Right Turns

186 **"I want to be remembered"**: Dorothy Height, quoted in "Celebrating Women—The Life and Legacy of Dorothy Height," YWCA St. Paul, www.ywcastpaul.org/celebrating-dorothy-height.

191 **"We cannot change the world"**: Richard Rohr, "There Is Nothing to Regret (God Uses Everything in Our Favor)," Center for Action and Contemplation, June 12, 2017, https://cac.org/nothing-regret-god-uses-everything-favor-2017-06-12.

191 **"spooky actions at a distance."**: Albert Einstein, "3 March, 1947," in *The Born-Einstein Letters 1916–1955: Friendship, Politics and Physics in Uncertain Times* (New York: Macmillan, 2005), 155.

192 **in every entangled pair of particles**: Paul Sutter, "What Is Quantum Entanglement?," Live Science, May 26, 2021, www.livescience.com/what-is-quantum-entanglement.html.

193 **"the disempowerment of members"**: Lea Ypi, "Structural Injustice and the Place of Attachment," *Journal of Practical Ethics*, www.jpe.ox.ac.uk/papers/structural-injustice-and-the-place-of-attachment.

194 **"The unintended consequences of the confluence"**: Iris Marion Young, "Political Responsibility and Structural Injustice" (Lindley Lecture, University of Kansas, May 5, 2003), 6, https://kuscholarworks.ku.edu/bitstream/handle/1808/12416/politicalresponsibilityandstructuralinjustice-2003.pdf?sequence=1.

195 **"Structural injustices are harms"**: Young, "Political Responsibility," 7.

195 **a mother living in Akron, Ohio, was arrested**: Annie Lowrey, "Her Only Crime Was Helping Her Kids," *The Atlantic*, September 13, 2019, www.theatlantic.com/ideas/archive/2019/09/her-only-crime-was-helping-her-kid/597979.

196 **almost one hundred thousand miles of blood vessels**: "Blood Vessels," The Franklin Institute, www.fi.edu/heart/blood-vessels.

199 **"before the 1830s, education was largely"**: Robert P. Murphy, "The Origins of the Public School," Foundation for Economic Education, July 1, 1998, https://fee.org/articles/the-origins-of-the-public-school.

199 **"The distinction between private and public schools"**: Murphy, "Origins of the Public School."

199 **"huge influx of poor, non-Protestant immigrants"**: Murphy, "Origins of the Public School."

Notes

Epilogue

201 **"While the tale of how we suffer"**: James Baldwin, "Sonny's Blues," in *Classics of Modern Fiction: Twelve Short Novels,* 4th ed., ed. Irving Howe (San Diego: Harcourt Brace Jovanovich, 1986), 642, https://archive.org/details/classicsofmodern00irvi/mode/2up.

About the Author

MICHAEL PHILLIPS is passionate about helping people live a better life. His determination to drive social change with lasting transformational benefits to society has led him to become an innovator and thought leader in social entrepreneurship and education. He is the founder of LifePrep and currently serves as the chief engagement and fulfillment officer for the T. D. Jakes Foundation.

As an author and inspirational speaker, Michael has become a champion for children and families around the world. He is the chairman of 50CAN, and he serves as a board member of KuriosEd. His powerful story and message of collateral hope has transformed many lives and helped revitalize communities. Michael Phillips and his wife, Dr. Anita Phillips, reside in Dallas, Texas.

About the Type

This book was set in Sabon, a typeface designed by the well-known German typographer Jan Tschichold (1902–74). Sabon's design is based upon the original letter forms of sixteenth-century French type designer Claude Garamond and was created specifically to be used for three sources: foundry type for hand composition, Linotype, and Monotype. Tschichold named his typeface for the famous Frankfurt typefounder Jacques Sabon (c. 1520–80).

T.D. JAKES
F O U N D A T I O N

Michael Phillips is working in communities nationwide to disassemble the systems that require reform to create generational equity. He has partnered with the T.D. Jakes Foundation to expand those efforts. And you can too.

Michael encourages you to donate to the foundation, a nonprofit working to dismantle barriers to opportunity, champion programs that advance racial and gender equity, and support companies in creating more diverse, inclusive, and equitable workplaces.

Your donation will help to support the foundation's Urban Reentry Initiative that aims to dramatically reduce recidivism rates among former offenders through coaching, housing assistance, job training and placement, education, healthcare, and transportation.

Support the T.D. Jakes Foundation by donating at

tdjfoundation.org